FRENCH

COOKING MADE EASY

ASSISTANT FOOD EDITOR
BARBARA NORTHWOOD

HOME ECONOMISTS
JOHN ALLEN, WENDY BERECRY,
JANE CLEARY, SUE HIPWELL,
JO-ANNE POWER

FOOD STYLISTS
JACQUI HING
CAROLYN FIENBERG

EDITORIAL ASSISTANT
DENISE PRENTICE

KITCHEN ASSISTANT
AMY WONG

EDITOR
SUE WENDT

DEPUTY EDITOR
ENID MORRISON

PRODUCTION EDITOR
MARYANNE BLACKER

SUB-EDITOR
MARY-ANNE DANAHER

CREATIVE DIRECTOR
BROOKE STANFORD

ART DIRECTOR
ROBBYLEE PHELAN

LAYOUT ARTIST
KAREN HARBOROW

EDITORIAL ASSISTANT
DIANNE AGOSTINI

PHOTOGRAPHY
PAUL CLARKE
ASHLEY MACKEVICIUS
ANDRE MARTIN
GEORGIA MOXHAM

PUBLISHER
RICHARD WALSH

ASSOCIATE PUBLISHER
SALLY MILNER

French cooking traditionally conjures up images of food that is deliciously rich in flavour, stylish in presentation and complex in its preparation. We have selected well known French dishes and adapted them slightly to suit Australian tastes and lifestyles. We have also simplified them with the inclusion of essential step by step instructions. The results are sure to please. Bon appetit!

Pamela Clark
FOOD EDITOR

ENTREES
PAGE 2

MAIN COURSES
PAGE 30

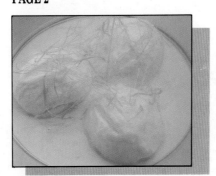

DESSERTS
PAGE 70

SWEET TREATS
PAGE 114

PRODUCED BY THE AUSTRALIAN WOMEN'S WEEKLY SPECIAL PROJECTS DIVISION.
Typeset by Photoset Computer Service Pty Ltd, Sydney, Australia.
Printed by Dai Nippon Co Ltd, Tokyo, Japan.
Published by Australian Consolidated Press, 54 Park Street, Sydney.
Distributed by Network Distribution Company, 54 Park Street, Sydney.
Distributed in U.K. by T. B. Clarke (UK) Limited (0604) 23 0941

French Cooking Made Easy.
    ISBN 0 949892 36 X.
    1. Cookery, French. I. Title: Australian Women's Weekly.
641.5944

BRIOCHE

Brioche is the richest of all yeast breads, incorporating butter and eggs. They make a wonderful entree, or a delicious treat for brunch. Individual brioche can be prepared the day before, up to placing the dough into the moulds; cover, refrigerate overnight. Allow the brioche to return to room temperature, proceed as below. This recipe is enough for 12 individual ½ cup moulds. If only 6 moulds are available; cook 6 brioche; remaining dough can be left covered in the refrigerator until ready to cook the remaining brioche. Brioche is best eaten warm so that its rich buttery flavour and fine texture can be fully appreciated. We served ours with creamy scrambled eggs flavoured with smoked salmon. Baked brioche can be frozen for up to 2 months. This recipe is unsuitable to microwave.

15g compressed yeast
1 teaspoon sugar
½ cup warm water
4 cups plain flour
1 teaspoon salt
2 tablespoons sugar, extra
4 eggs, lightly beaten
185g butter, softened
1 egg yolk, extra
¼ cup cream
FILLING
60g packaged cream cheese
30g butter
⅓ cup cream
3 eggs
100g smoked salmon, chopped
1 tablespoon chopped fresh chives

1 Cream yeast with the 1 teaspoon sugar in a small bowl, stir in warm water, cover, stand in a warm place for about 10 minutes or until mixture is foamy. Sift flour, salt and extra sugar into a large bowl; make well in centre, stir in combined eggs and yeast mixture. Turn onto lightly floured surface; knead mixture for about 5 minutes or until dough is smooth and elastic. Dough should be fairly dry now.

2 Work butter in gradually; butter should be quite soft. Continue adding small pieces of butter to the dough until all the butter is incorporated, this should take about 5 minutes. Knead dough further 10 minutes, or until smooth, shiny and elastic.

3 Place dough in a greased bowl, cover with plastic wrap, stand in a warm place for about 1 hour or until dough is doubled in bulk. Knock dough back, knead until smooth. Divide dough into 12 portions. Grease moulds (½ cup capacity). Remove a quarter of the dough from each portion. Mould the larger portions into rounds, place in moulds. Shape smaller portions of dough into rounds. Brush dough in moulds with combined extra egg yolk and cream. Place small rounds of dough on top of dough in moulds.

4 Using a wooden skewer, push dough from the top of the small round through to the base of the mould. This ensures that the small round will stay in position during cooking. Brush with remaining egg yolk and

Tiles: from Country Floors; plate: from The Bay Tree; cutlery: from Studio Haus

cream, stand in a warm place for about 15 minutes or until brioche are doubled in size. Bake in moderately hot oven for 10 minutes, reduce heat to moderate, bake further 10 minutes or until brioche sound hollow when tapped with finger. Turn out of moulds immediately onto wire rack.

5 Cut tops from each brioche, scoop out a little of the dough to allow space for the filling.

6 **Filling:** Melt cream cheese and butter in small frying pan, stir in combined cream and eggs, cook, stirring, over low heat until just beginning to set, stir in salmon and chives, place filling in brioche; serve immediately.
  Makes 12.

ENTREES

3

reduce heat, cover, simmer gently for 3 hours. Strain, cool, refrigerate overnight. Scoop fat from top of stock.

2 Heat butter and oil in large saucepan, add the sliced onions, cook over low heat until onions are golden brown and soft; this will take about 20 minutes, stir occasionally. Add flour, stir over heat 1 minute.

3 Add wine and 5 cups of the stock, stir constantly over heat until mixture boils and thickens. Reduce heat, simmer covered 10 minutes.

FRENCH ONION SOUP

The browning of the onions and a good beef stock are the important parts of this recipe. This soup is best made and served immediately. Any leftover stock can be frozen for several months. This recipe is unsuitable to freeze or microwave.

375g gravy beef, chopped
2 onions, chopped
2 bay leaves
½ cup parsley sprigs
2 teaspoons whole black peppercorns
2 litres (8 cups) water
30g butter
1 tablespoon oil
4 large onions, thinly sliced, extra
¼ cup plain flour
¼ cup dry red wine
1 small French bread stick
45g butter, extra
2 cloves garlic, crushed
¼ cup grated parmesan cheese

1 To make the stock: Combine beef, the chopped onions, bay leaves, parsley, peppercorns and water in large saucepan, bring stock to the boil,

4 Slice the bread. Melt extra butter, add garlic, brush onto each side of the bread. Place onto an ungreased oven tray, bake in moderate oven for about 20 minutes or until bread is dry and crisp. Sprinkle slices with parmesan cheese, bake further 5 minutes. Place slices in serving dishes, top with hot soup; serve immediately.
Serves 6.

Table: Wentworth Antiques; china: Longchamp from Studio Haus

This is our favourite version of this recipe. It must be made and served immediately, as seafood does not reheat successfully. This recipe is unsuitable to freeze or microwave.

6 small uncooked blue
    swimmer crabs
2 tablespoons oil
4 cloves garlic, crushed
2 onions, chopped
¼ cup tomato paste
½ cup dry white wine
2 x 400g cans tomatoes
½ teaspoon turmeric
2 bay leaves
2 teaspoons sugar
1 cup water
1 kg fish fillets, chopped
500g uncooked king prawns, shelled
250g scallops
250g calamari rings

1 Remove triangular flap from under-side of each crab, remove the hard top shell and grey fibrous tissue; wash crab. Crack nippers slightly, chop down centre of each crab to separate body into 2 pieces.

BOUILLABAISSE

tomatoes, turmeric, bay leaves, sugar and water. Bring to the boil, reduce heat, simmer uncovered 10 minutes.

2 Heat oil in large deep frying pan, add garlic and onions, cook, stirring, until the onions are soft. Stir in tomato paste, wine, undrained crushed

3 Add crab and fish to tomato mixture, bring to the boil, reduce heat, simmer covered 5 minutes.

4 Devein prawns leaving tails intact. Remove vein from scallops. Stir prawns, scallops and calamari into tomato mixture, bring to boil, reduce heat, simmer few minutes or until prawns are cooked. Serve the bouillabaisse immediately.
Serves 6.

VICHYSSOISE

Soup can be made and stored covered in refrigerator up to 2 days before serving. This recipe is unsuitable to freeze or microwave.

No. 13 chicken
2 litres (8 cups) water
2 onions, chopped
2 bay leaves
2 teaspoons whole black peppercorns
2kg (about 8 large) potatoes
2 leeks
300ml carton cream

bay leaves and peppercorns. Bring to the boil, reduce heat, cover, simmer for 2 hours, strain, reserve stock. You will need 1½ litres (6 cups) of stock for this recipe. Remaining stock can be cooled and frozen for future use.

3 Combine potatoes, leeks and reserved stock in large saucepan, bring to the boil, reduce heat, simmer covered 40 minutes.

4 Blend or process soup until smooth; strain. Return to saucepan, stir in cream, reheat gently without boiling. Serve topped with chives. Serves 6.

1 Cut chicken in half, combine in large saucepan with water, onions,

2 Peel and roughly chop potatoes. Trim leaves from leeks, chop white part roughly; wash, drain well.

This soup is based on fresh crab. The recipe can be made up to 1 day before serving; store covered in refrigerator. Reheat gently without boiling; add fresh chopped dill just before serving. This recipe is unsuitable to freeze or microwave.

4 uncooked blue swimmer crabs
2 litres (8 cups) water
60g butter
1 onion, chopped
½ cup dry white wine
¼ cup brandy
2 tomatoes, peeled, chopped
⅓ cup rice
2 teaspoons tomato paste
½ cup cream
2 egg yolks
2 tablespoons chopped fresh dill

CRAB BISQUE

1 Remove triangular flap from underside of each crab. Insert a knife through slit where flap has been removed, to separate the hard top shell from the body of the crab.

2 Remove grey fibrous tissue, wash crab. Using fingers, remove meat from shell. Remove legs and nippers.

3 Using a meat mallet, crack shells on legs, carefully remove meat.

4 Place crab shells in large saucepan with water. Bring to the boil, reduce heat, simmer uncovered 30 minutes or until stock is slightly reduced. Strain shells through fine sieve; discard shells. Reserve stock; you will need 1½ litres (6 cups) of stock.

5 Heat butter in large saucepan, add onion, cook, stirring, until onion is soft. Add combined wine and brandy, bring to the boil, add tomatoes, rice, tomato paste and reserved stock. Bring to the boil, reduce heat, simmer uncovered 20 minutes. Stir in combined cream and egg yolks. Blend or process soup until smooth. Reheat soup without boiling, add chopped crab meat and dill.
Serves 6.

VOL AU VENTS

Vol au Vents make a hearty first course; each of the fillings is sufficient for 6 cases. Unfilled Vol au Vent cases can be stored in an airtight container for up to 1 week, or frozen for up to 2 months. To serve, place the Vol au Vents on an oven tray, fill, reheat in moderate oven, uncovered for about 10 minutes. This recipe is unsuitable to microwave.

375g packet puff pastry
1 egg yolk
FILLING
60g butter
2 tablespoons plain flour
⅔ cup milk
⅓ cup cream
⅓ cup dry white wine
2 teaspoons chopped parsley

1 Have pastry at room temperature, roll out on a lightly floured surface to a rectangle measuring 25cm x

35cm; make sure corners are as square as possible. Pastry should be the same thickness all over. Using a 5cm cutter, cut out 6 rounds from half the pastry as shown, leave space around each circle of pastry to cut larger rounds as shown. Brush uncut half of pastry lightly with water.

2 Fold pastry in half, pastry with cut rounds is now on top of uncut pastry. Using a 7cm cutter, cut out larger rounds around smaller rounds; be sure to centralise large cutter around smaller rounds, before cutting through the 2 layers of pastry. Place vol au vents on oven tray, refrigerate overnight. This is important to ensure the vol au vents

keep their shape when cooking. Glaze around top rims with beaten egg yolk, make sure it does not run over sides of pastry or pastry will not rise evenly.

3 Suspend a wire rack over vol au vent cases, as shown; rack will need to be 3cm higher than the oven tray. We used 2 cutters to support rack. Bake in a very hot oven for 5 minutes, reduce heat to moderate, bake further 5 minutes, remove wire rack, continue to bake further 5 minutes or until golden brown. Remove cases to wire rack to cool.

4 **Filling:** Melt butter in saucepan, stir in flour, stir over heat 1 minute, gradually stir in combined milk, cream and wine, stir constantly over heat until sauce boils and thickens, reduce heat, add parsley and desired filling, simmer, stirring, for 2 minutes.

FILLINGS
ASPARAGUS
340g can asparagus spears, drained
⅔ cup grated tasty cheese
Chop asparagus, combine with cheese; mix well.
MUSHROOM AND HAM
310g can champignons, drained
100g leg ham, chopped
Halve champignons, combine with ham; mix well.
OYSTER
12 oysters
1 teaspoon grated lemon rind
2 green shallots, chopped
Combine all ingredients.
Makes 6.

Background table: Kerry Trollope Antiques; placemat: Balmain Linen & Lace; plate: Studio Haus

This pâté can be made up to 1 day ahead of serving. This recipe is unsuitable to freeze.

1 butter lettuce
15g butter
3 teaspoons plain flour
2 tablespoons milk
2 tablespoons mayonnaise
1 tablespoon cream
2 teaspoons tomato paste
1 teaspoon lemon juice
½ teaspoon dry mustard
170g can crab, drained
60g packaged cream cheese
1 avocado, chopped
1 clove garlic, crushed
2 teaspoons lemon juice, extra
¼ teaspoon tabasco
125g packet cream cheese, extra

LAYERED CRAB AND AVOCADO PATE

1 Drop lettuce leaves into pan of boiling water, drain immediately. Place into bowl of iced water; drain immediately. Line 6 individual ½ cup dishes with lettuce leaves.

2 Melt butter in saucepan, stir in flour, stir over heat 1 minute. Gradually stir in combined milk, mayonnaise and cream, stir constantly over heat until mixture boils and thickens. Remove from heat, stir in tomato paste, lemon juice and mustard, cover, cool to room temperature. Stir crab into sauce. Process crab mixture and cream cheese until smooth. Spoon crab mixture evenly into lettuce-lined dishes, refrigerate for about 1 hour.

3 Process remaining ingredients until smooth, stopping occasionally to scrape down the side of the bowl.

4 Spoon avocado mixture evenly over crab mixture. Top with reserved lettuce leaves to completely enclose the pâtés in lettuce. Refrigerate several hours or overnight.
Serves 6.

CHICKEN LIVER AND PORT PATE

This pâté can be frozen for up to 2 weeks without the gelatine topping. The recipe can be prepared up to 2 days ahead of serving. Serve with toast or Melba Toast (see opposite page) if desired.

500g chicken livers
⅓ cup port
90g butter
1 small onion, finely chopped
1 clove garlic, crushed
⅓ cup cream
¼ teaspoon ground nutmeg
½ teaspoon ground thyme
1 teaspoon gelatine
½ chicken stock cube
½ cup water

1 Trim and wash livers, cut in half. Place livers into a small bowl with the port; stand 2 hours. Strain livers, reserve liquid. Melt half the butter in a frying pan, add onion and garlic, stir over heat until onion is soft. Add livers to pan, stir over heat for a few minutes or until livers change colour. Add reserved liquid, simmer mixture uncovered 1 minute.

2 Melt remaining butter. Blend or process liver mixture, cream, nutmeg and thyme until smooth. Add melted butter while motor is operating. Process until smooth. Pour into serving dish, cover, refrigerate 2 hours.

3 Sprinkle gelatine and crumbled stock cube over water, dissolve over hot water (or microwave on HIGH for about 30 seconds), cool to room temperature. Arrange bay leaves and strips of canned pimiento on pâté, carefully pour gelatine mixture over pâté; refrigerate overnight.

Serves 4.

MELBA TOAST

Melba Toast or Fairy Bread has a crunchy texture which makes it a good accompaniment to mousses, pâtés and terrines. An electric or finely serrated knife makes slicing easier. The finer the slices the more it curls during baking. Toast may be stored in an airtight container for up to 2 weeks. You will need 1 loaf of square, unsliced white bread. This recipe is not suitable to freeze or microwave.

1 Cut loaf in half to allow for easier handling. Remove all crusts from bread. Cut each loaf diagonally in half, giving 4 triangular pieces of bread.

2 Place widest side of triangle on board, cut into wafer-thin slices. Place triangles onto ungreased oven trays in a single layer. Bake in slow oven for about 30 minutes or until bread is crisp and lightly browned.

SMOKED SALMON PATE

This delicious pâté is quick and easy to prepare; it can be made up to 2 days ahead of serving. Keep covered in refrigerator. Smoked salmon pieces or offcuts can be bought from some delicatessens; it can also be bought frozen. This recipe is not suitable to freeze.

300g smoked salmon
125g unsalted butter
1 small onion, finely chopped
2 teaspoons lemon juice
1 teaspoon French mustard
2 tablespoons cream
¼ teaspoon tabasco
1 teaspoon drained capers
Process all ingredients until smooth, stopping occasionally to scrape down the side of the bowl.

Spoon mixture into serving dish. Smooth top of pâté with knife or spatula. Refrigerate several hours or overnight until firm.
Serves 4 to 6.

Plate, linen: Studio Haus; knife: Mikasa; tiles: Fred Pazotti

2 Remove skin and bones from the salmon. Add salmon to blender with cream and mayonnaise, blend until smooth. Press mixture through sieve into bowl.

3 Sprinkle gelatine over water in small jug, dissolve over hot water (or microwave on HIGH for about 30 seconds). Stir a little of the salmon mixture into the gelatine mixture, stir into salmon mixture with dill.

4 Beat egg whites in small bowl until soft peaks from, fold into salmon mixture. Pour into lightly oiled 20cm savarin mould, refrigerate several hours or until set.
Serves 6.

SALMON MOUSSE

Salmon Mousse makes a deliciously light first course. Serve it with toast or Melba Toast (see page 11). It can be made, covered and refrigerated for up to 2 days before serving. This recipe is not suitable to freeze.

2 tablespoons lemon juice
1 tablespoon white vinegar
3 eggs, separated
125g butter, melted
440g can red salmon, drained
½ cup thickened cream
¼ cup mayonnaise
3 teaspoons gelatine
2 tablespoons water
2 teaspoons chopped fresh dill

1 Blend or process lemon juice, vinegar and egg yolks until pale lemon in colour. With motor operating, gradually pour in hot, bubbling butter.

Roulade can be made several hours ahead. Cover roulade with foil, reheat in a moderate oven for about 10 minutes. You will need to buy 500g of watercress for this recipe. The lemon sauce is best made just before serving time. This roulade will serve about 6 people; it is unsuitable to freeze or microwave.

60g butter
⅓ cup plain flour
1 cup milk
⅓ cup grated parmesan cheese
2 cups chopped fresh watercress
4 eggs, separated
FILLING
100g packaged cream cheese
¼ cup sour cream
2 bacon rashers, finely chopped
100g mushrooms, finely chopped
LEMON SAUCE
4 egg yolks
30g butter
1 teaspoon grated lemon rind
tiny pinch saffron
½ cup sour cream
2 teaspoons lemon juice.

WATERCRESS ROULADE

1 Heat butter in saucepan, add flour, cook, stirring 1 minute, gradually stir in milk, stir constantly over heat until mixture boils and thickens. Stir in cheese, egg yolks and watercress, transfer mixture to a large bowl. Beat egg whites until soft peaks form, fold lightly into watercress mixture.

2 Pour mixture into greased and lined Swiss roll pan (base measures 25cm x 30cm). Bake in moderately hot oven for about 20 minutes or until roulade is golden brown.

3 Quickly turn roulade onto wire rack covered with tea towel; carefully remove lining paper. Spread with cream cheese mixture, then bacon mixture. Use the towel to help roll the roulade from the short side.

4 Filling: Have cream cheese at room temperature, beat in small bowl with electric mixer until smooth, stir in sour cream. Add bacon and mushrooms to small frying pan, cook, stirring, until bacon is crisp.

Lemon Sauce: Combine egg yolks, butter, lemon rind and saffron in top of double saucepan or bowl, whisk over hot water until butter is melted. Gradually whisk in sour cream, whisk constantly until sauce is slightly thickened, whisk in lemon juice.

FRESH ASPARAGUS WITH HOLLANDAISE SAUCE

Hollandaise sauce can be whisked by hand or a simpler version can be made in a blender or food processor. Be sure to warm the egg yolks very slowly and add the butter gradually. Hollandaise sauce can rarely be served hotter than lukewarm; reheating usually causes curdling. If sauce curdles, beat 1 egg yolk with ¼ teaspoon of dry mustard in a bowl, then gradually whisk in curdled sauce. Leftover hollandaise sauce can be stored in an airtight container in the refrigerator for up to 2 days. To reheat, heat 2 tablespoons of hollandaise in a saucepan over a very low heat or in a bowl over hot water. Gradually beat in the remaining sauce. Variations on the classic hollandaise appear at right.

¼ cup water
2 tablespoons lemon juice
1 bay leaf
2 green shallots, finely chopped
1 teaspoon whole black peppercorns
3 egg yolks
185g butter, chopped

1 Combine water, lemon juice, bay leaf, shallots and peppercorns in small frying pan. Bring to the boil, reduce heat, simmer until liquid is reduced to 2 tablespoons; strain and reserve liquid; cool.

2 Combine egg yolks and lemon mixture in bowl or top of double saucepan over simmering water; do not allow water to touch base of bowl or top saucepan. Whisk mixture constantly until thickened.

3 Whisk in a couple of cubes of butter at a time; whisk until butter is incorporated before adding more butter. Continue until all the butter is used. (This will take about 10 minutes of constant whisking.) Hollandaise should be just pourable. If it is too thick to pour, stir in 1 to 2 tablespoons of hot water.

4 Trim ends of asparagus so that they are all an even length, then if asparagus spears are thick, use a vegetable peeler to scrape the end parts of the stems well.

Place asparagus on wire rack over water in baking dish, bring to the boil, reduce heat, simmer covered 2 minutes or until just tender. Drain the asparagus, serve warm or cold with hollandaise sauce.

Caper Hollandaise: Rinse 2 tablespoons of capers under cold water; drain on absorbent paper. Chop capers finely and stir into sauce. Serve with fish, eggs and poultry.

Lemon Hollandaise: Add 1 tablespoon grated lemon rind to sauce. Serve with seafood or chicken.

Mousseline Hollandaise: Fold ¼ cup whipped cream and 1 firmly beaten egg white into sauce. Serve with poached fish, vegetables or egg dishes.

Mustard Hollandaise: Add 2 tablespoons French mustard to sauce. Serve with grilled fish or chicken.

Herb Hollandaise: Add 2 tablespoons finely chopped fresh mixed herbs, such as parsley, chives, mint or basil into sauce. Serve with grilled meat, chicken or vegetables.

BLENDER HOLLANDAISE

The amount of butter used in the blender is only about half the amount the egg yolks could absorb if the sauce were made by hand. If more than the 125g of butter is used, the sauce will be too thick. If sauce is too thick to pour, stir in 1 to 2 tablespoons hot water.

3 egg yolks
2 tablespoons lemon juice
125g butter, melted

Combine yolks and lemon juice in blender or food processor, blend 5 seconds. With motor operating, pour in hot bubbling butter into egg mixture in slow steady stream (it should take about 15 seconds). Omit the milky residue at the bottom of the saucepan.

Table: Appley Hoare Antiques. china: Limoges Contrast de per Spook from Studio Haus: spoon: Studio Haus

2 Spread half the chicken filling into dish, top with spinach filling, then remaining chicken filling.

3 Top with reserved spinach leaves, cover dish with foil.

SPINACH AND CHICKEN TERRINE

You will need to cook ¼ cup of rice for this recipe. This terrine can be made up to a day before. If serving cold, it will serve at least 6 people. It will not reheat successfully. This recipe is unsuitable to freeze or microwave.

1 bunch English spinach
CHICKEN FILLING
15g butter
1 onion, finely chopped
2 bacon rashers, chopped
2 teaspoons curry powder
4 chicken breast fillets, chopped
¼ cup cream
2 eggs, lightly beaten
SPINACH FILLING
1 bunch English spinach
15g butter
1 clove garlic, crushed
¾ cup cooked rice
2 tablespoons cream
1 egg, lightly beaten
¼ teaspoon ground nutmeg

TOMATO SAUCE
3 ripe tomatoes, chopped
1 onion, chopped
1 tablespoon red wine vinegar
½ teaspoon sugar

1 Remove stalks from spinach, rinse spinach. Boil, steam or microwave spinach until tender, drain well. Line base and sides of greased ovenproof dish (6 cup capacity) with spinach leaves, reserving a few of the leaves for top of terrine.

4 Place terrine in baking dish with enough hot water to come halfway up sides of dish. Bake in moderate oven for about 1 hour or until set. Remove dish from water, stand 5 minutes. Remove foil, invert terrine onto serving plate. Serve warm or cold with tomato sauce.

Chicken Filling: Melt butter in frying pan, add onion, bacon and curry powder, cook, stirring, until onion is soft. Process onion mixture, chicken, cream and eggs until smooth.

Spinach Filling: Remove stalks from spinach, rinse spinach, chop finely. Melt butter in saucepan, add garlic and spinach, stir over heat until spinach is wilted (or microwave on HIGH for about 2 minutes). Drain, press out as much moisture as possible. Combine spinach, rice, cream, egg and nutmeg in bowl, mix well.

Tomato Sauce: Combine all ingredients in saucepan, bring to the boil, reduce heat, simmer covered 10 minutes, stirring occasionally (or microwave on HIGH about 4 minutes). Blend or process until smooth; strain. Reheat before serving.

China and cutlery: The Bay Tree; linen: Studio Haus; tiles: Fred Pazotti

This terrine is best made as close to serving time as possible. It will serve at least 6 people as an entree. This recipe is unsuitable to freeze or microwave.

500g scallops
60g butter
2 green shallots, chopped
2 tablespoons brandy
500g white fish fillets
1 cup stale breadcrumbs
¼ cup milk
3 eggs, separated
¼ cup cream
500g uncooked prawns, shelled
TOMATO SAUCE
15g butter
2 green shallots, chopped
¼ cup tomato paste
1 tablespoon brandy
½ cup dry white wine
1 cup cream
1 teaspoon sugar
1 tablespoon drained canned green
   peppercorns

SEAFOOD TERRINE

1 Remove coral from half the scallops, reserve coral. Heat butter in large frying pan, add the half of scallops with coral, reserved coral, half the shallots and half the brandy; cook 1 minute, stirring constantly. Combine fish, remaining scallops, remaining brandy, remaining shallots, breadcrumbs and combined milk, egg yolks and cream in processor. Process until smooth, transfer to large bowl; refrigerate 30 minutes.

2 Beat egg whites until soft peaks form, fold into fish mixture, refrigerate further 30 minutes.

3 Spread half the fish mixture into a 5 cup capacity ovenproof dish, cover with cooked scallop mixture, top with a third of the remaining fish mixture; cover with prawns and top with remaining fish mixture.

4 Place in baking dish with enough hot water to come half way up sides of ovenproof dish. Bake covered in slow oven for about 1 hour or until firm. Remove dish from water, stand terrine 30 minutes before serving.
Tomato Sauce: Melt butter in frying pan, add shallots, cook 1 minute; stir in remaining ingredients, bring to the boil, reduce heat, simmer for about 5 minutes or until reduced by a quarter; stir occasionally during cooking.

Plate: Sasaki from Dansab; cutlery: Mikasa; linen: Studio Haus

PORK AND VEAL TERRINE

Terrine is best made and refrigerated at least 24 hours before use, but can be made up to 1 week ahead; store in refrigerator. It will serve at least 6 people as an entree. Sauce can be made at the same time as terrine. This recipe is unsuitable to freeze or microwave.

1kg pork and veal mince
2 onions, chopped
6 bacon rashers, chopped
2 cloves garlic, crushed
2 eggs, lightly beaten
2 cups stale white breadcrumbs
2 tablespoons brandy
½ cup fruit chutney
¾ cup shelled pistachio nuts
2 chicken breast fillets
125g sliced leg ham
PASTRY
2 cups plain flour
1 cup self-raising flour
185g butter
2 tablespoons lemon juice
¼ cup water, approximately

CUMBERLAND SAUCE
1 lemon
2 oranges
2 green shallots, chopped
2 tablespoons red currant jelly
¼ cup port
½ teaspoon French mustard
pinch cayenne pepper

1 Process mince, onions and bacon until fine. Stir in garlic, eggs, breadcrumbs, brandy, chutney and nuts. Cut chicken and ham into strips. Press

one-third of the mixture into loaf pan (14cm x 21cm), top with chicken and ham strips. Spread with remaining

mince mixture. Cover with foil, bake in moderate oven for about 2 hours or until firm to touch.

Turn terrine onto a wire rack to drain for 30 minutes. Return terrine to loaf pan, cover with plastic wrap. Place a weight on top (a brick is ideal) to compact terrine; refrigerate overnight.

2 **Pastry:** Sift flours into bowl, rub in butter. Add lemon juice and just enough water to make ingredients cling together. Knead gently on lightly floured surface until smooth, cover, refrigerate 30 minutes. Roll pastry to a 40cm x 50cm rectangle.

3 Place terrine in centre of pastry. Cut out corners, as shown. Bring edges of pastry together at top. Press all edges together firmly. Turn terrine over, place on oven tray. Decorate top of terrine with shapes cut from remaining pastry; brush with a little milk. Bake in moderately hot oven for 40 minutes or until golden brown, cool to room temperature before refrigerating. Serve terrine with cumberland sauce.
Cumberland Sauce: Using a vegetable peeler, remove rind from lemon and one of the oranges, being careful not to remove any white pith; cut rind into very thin strips about 2cm long. Place rind in small saucepan, cover with water, bring to the boil, boil uncovered 3 minutes, drain. Squeeze juice from lemon and oranges; you will need 2 tablespoons of lemon juice and ½ cup orange juice. Combine juices, rind, shallots, jelly, port, mustard and cayenne in saucepan, bring to boil, boil 2 minutes; cool before using.

Tiles: Country Floors; china: Longchamp from Studio Haus; board: Scanada Agencies; knife: Appley Hoare Antiques

Duck livers should be soaked overnight in salted water; these livers are ideal for terrines as they give a smooth texture. Terrine can be made several days in advance and kept covered in refrigerator. It will serve at least 6 people. This recipe is unsuitable to freeze or microwave.

750g duck livers
125g butter
2 cloves garlic, crushed
1 cup stale white breadcrumbs
½ cup orange juice
4 eggs
½ cup cream
¼ cup Grand Marnier
1 orange
¼ cup sugar
¼ cup water

DUCK AND ORANGE TERRINE

1 Soak trimmed livers in salted water overnight in refrigerator; drain, rinse under cold water; drain well. Melt butter in saucepan, add garlic, cook, stirring, 1 minute, remove from heat, stir in crumbs, then orange juice. Process livers until smooth.

2 Combine crumb mixture and livers; push mixture through a sieve.

3 Combine eggs, cream, Grand Marnier and liver mixture in a large bowl, whisk until smooth. Pour mixture into a well greased, base lined rectangular ovenproof dish (4 cup capacity); cover with greased foil. Place terrine in a baking dish with enough hot water to come halfway up sides of the dish. Bake in moderate oven for about 1 hour or until firm to touch. Remove from oven, cool to room temperature. Refrigerate covered until 1 hour before turning onto serving plate.

4 Use vegetable peeler to remove rind from orange, cut rind into strips. Remove white pith from orange. Cut orange into thin slices, then into segments. Place orange on terrine. Combine sugar and water in small saucepan, stir over heat without boiling until the sugar is dissolved. Bring to the boil, reduce heat, add rind, simmer 3 minutes without stirring, cool.

Remove rind from syrup, place on terrine, brush terrine lightly with a little of the syrup.

QUICHE LORRAINE

Quiche Lorraine is a savoury flan which originated in the area of Lorraine in France. This is a good basic recipe for quiche; serve a small wedge with a light salad for a first course. It can be served warm, hot or cold. The pastry case can be "baked blind", cooled and stored in an airtight container for about a week. If weather is humid, store in refrigerator. The quiche is at its best freshly made, then baked, but for convenience it can be frozen. We found the best results were obtained by placing the filling into the baked pastry case, still in the flan tin. Freeze uncooked quiche uncovered for 1 hour (flan tin can be removed at this stage if desired), wrap quiche tightly, freeze for up to 4 weeks. To bake: Place uncovered frozen quiche (in its flan tin) on oven tray, bake in moderate oven for about 50 minutes. This recipe is unsuitable to microwave.

PASTRY
1¾ cups plain flour
155g butter
1 egg yolk
2 teaspoons lemon juice, approximately
FILLING
1 onion, finely chopped
3 bacon rashers, chopped
3 eggs
300ml carton cream
½ cup milk
¾ cup grated tasty cheese

1 **Pastry:** Sift flour into bowl; rub in butter. Add egg yolk and enough lemon juice to make ingredients cling together. Knead gently on lightly floured surface until smooth, cover, refrigerate 30 minutes. Roll pastry large enough to line a deep 23cm flan tin. If weather is hot and pastry is difficult to handle, roll pastry between 2 pieces plastic wrap or greaseproof or baking paper. Lift pastry into flan tin, gently ease pastry into side of tin; do not stretch the pastry or it will shrink during the cooking.

2 Use the rolling pin to trim the edges of pastry neatly. Place flan on oven tray for easier handling.

3 Cover pastry with greaseproof or baking paper, fill the cavity with dried beans of rice. This is called "baking blind". Bake in moderately hot oven for 10 minutes, remove paper and beans carefully, bake pastry for about further 10 minutes or until golden brown; cool to room temperature. Cool the beans or rice; store in an airtight container for future use when "baking blind".

4 **Filling:** Cook onion and bacon in frying pan until onion is soft; drain away excess fat, cool before spreading into pastry case.

5 Beat eggs in bowl with whisk, add cream, milk and cheese, whisk until just combined; pour into pastry case. Bake in moderate oven for about 35 minutes or until filling is set and brown.

6 Stand quiche 5 minutes before removing from tin as shown.

Wooden board: Scanada Agencies; louvre door, table, knife, egg basket: Appley Hoare Antiques

1 Whisk eggs and water in bowl until just combined.

2 Pour enough egg mixture into the heated, greased omelette pan to just cover base of pan. Cook over fairly high heat until eggs are almost set; an omelette should look set on the outside and creamy in the centre.

3 Place about a quarter of the filling over half the omelette.

4 Use a spatula to fold the omelette in half. Slide onto serving dish. Repeat with remaining egg mixture and filling to make 3 more omelettes.
Serves 4.

RATATOUILLE OMELETTE

A small tasty omelette is a pleasant entree to a meal; it is best to make and serve immediately as the cooking time is short and it does not reheat successfully. A little practice with the family will make you confident enough to do this for a dinner party; using 2 pans simultaneously will make it even easier. This recipe is not suitable to freeze or microwave.

Omelettes should be cooked in a heavy-based pan, the size doesn't matter although a shallow pan makes the omelette easier to remove from the pan to the plate. If using an aluminium pan it should be "seasoned" by heating the pan, then "polishing" it vigorously with some coarse cooking salt. A pad of absorbent paper makes an ideal "polisher". To season a copper pan, place a knob of butter into the pan, heat the pan until the butter burns. Use a pad of absorbent paper to wipe pan.

Some cooks prefer to keep a pan specially for omelettes, in this case washing is unnecessary, simply wipe out the pan properly with a pad of absorbent paper. Put the pan away carefully to avoid scratching the surface in any way.

6 eggs
2 tablespoons water
RATATOUILLE FILLING
1 tablespoon oil
1 clove garlic, crushed
1 small onion, finely chopped
2 canned anchovy fillets, drained
1 small eggplant, chopped
1 small red pepper, chopped
1 zucchini, chopped
400g can tomatoes

Ratatouille Filling: Heat oil in frying pan, add garlic and onion, stir over heat until onion is soft. Stir in chopped anchovies, eggplant, pepper, zucchini and undrained crushed tomatoes. Bring to the boil, reduce heat, simmer uncovered for about 10 minutes or until thick (or microwave on HIGH for about 5 minutes).

Table: Appley Hoare Antiques

Soufflés are quick and easy to make and look and taste impressive. The most important things are not to overbeat the egg whites and to serve the soufflés immediately because they will fall as they cool. To begin making soufflés ahead, simply prepare the whole recipe except for the folding in of the egg whites; that is up to the end of step 2. It is important to reheat the mixture to a warm temperature so it makes the egg whites easier to fold through the mixture. This recipe is unsuitable to freeze or microwave.

45g butter
1½ tablespoons plain flour
1 cup milk
3 eggs, separated
1 tablespoon chopped parsley
½ cup chopped fresh basil
1 tablespoon chopped fresh dill
1 tablespoon chopped fresh chives
SWEET PEPPER SAUCE
400g can sweet red peppers, drained
¼ cup cream
1 teaspoon sugar
2 teaspoons brandy

FRESH HERB SOUFFLES

1 Grease 6 soufflé dishes (½ cup capacity). Melt butter in saucepan, stir in flour; cook, stirring constantly, for 1 minute. Remove from heat, gradually stir in milk, stir until smooth. Return to heat, stir constantly until mixture boils and thickens.

2 Transfer to large bowl, cover surface with plastic wrap, cool to warm. Stir egg yolks, parsley, basil, dill and chives into bowl.

3 Beat egg whites in small bowl until soft peaks form, fold lightly into warm herb mixture. Place dishes onto oven tray, pour mixture evenly into dishes. Bake in moderately hot oven for about 15 minutes. Serve immediately with sauce.

Sweet Pepper Sauce: Blend or process peppers until pureed. Combine all ingredients in a frying pan, bring to the boil, reduce heat, simmer uncovered for about 2 minutes or until sauce is slightly thickened; strain before using. Reheat if necessary.

Serves 6.

2 Combine eggs, cream and cheese in bowl, whisk until well combined; stir in puree.

3 Pour pea mixture into 6 lightly greased ovenproof moulds (½ cup capacity). Cover each mould with a piece of lightly greased foil. Place moulds in baking dish with enough hot water to come halfway up sides of moulds. Bake in moderately slow oven for about 30 minutes or until timbales set. Remove moulds from dish, stand a few minutes before turning onto serving plates. Serve with mint hollandaise and tomato coulis; garnish with finely shredded shallots.

FRESH PEA TIMBALES

Timbales are a light start to a summertime dinner party. A timbale is similar to a soufflé or custard, and is cooked in a mould called a timbale; the mould is round with a straight sloping side. Timbales can be served warm or at room temperature and should be made on the day of serving. You will need about 3 cups of fresh peas for this recipe; frozen peas can also be used. The mint hollandaise and the tomato coulis can be made up to several hours before serving. Reheat sauces over a low heat; stir hollandaise constantly to prevent curdling; do not boil. This recipe is not suitable to freeze or microwave.

750g fresh peas, shelled
4 eggs
300g carton sour cream
¼ cup grated parmesan cheese

MINT HOLLANDAISE
¼ cup white vinegar
2 egg yolks
2 tablespoons chopped fresh mint
2 teaspoons lemon juice
125g butter, melted
TOMATO COULIS
1 tablespoon oil
1 clove garlic, crushed
1 onion, chopped
400g can tomatoes
½ teaspoon sugar

1 Steam, boil or microwave peas until just tender; drain. Blend or process peas until smooth. Push pea puree through a fine sieve; you will need about ½ cup puree.

4 **Mint Hollandaise:** Heat vinegar in small saucepan, boil until reduced by half. Blend or process egg yolks, mint, vinegar and lemon juice until smooth, gradually pour in hot, bubbling butter while motor is operating.
Tomato Coulis: Heat oil in saucepan, add garlic and onion, cook until onion is soft. Add undrained crushed tomatoes and sugar, cook, stirring, about 5 minutes. Blend or process until smooth, strain through fine sieve.
Serves 6.

Recipe can be made up to step 3 the day before required, cover, refrigerate. This recipe is unsuitable to freeze.

750g scallops
250g baby mushrooms
2 cups water
1 chicken stock cube
1 cup dry white wine
60g butter
2 tablespoons cornflour
¾ cup milk
½ cup cream
2 teaspoons lemon juice
30g butter, melted, extra
1 cup stale breadcrumbs
2 tablespoons grated parmesan
  cheese
4 green shallots, chopped

COQUILLES SAINT-JACQUES

mushrooms, water, crumbled stock cube and wine. Heat without boiling until scallops become opaque. Remove scallops and mushrooms (reserve stock), drain on absorbent paper. Strain stock, return stock to pan, boil rapidly until reduced to 1 cup.

microwave on HIGH 1 minute). Gradually stir in stock and milk, stir constantly over heat until mixture boils and thickens. Reduce heat, simmer, stirring, for 1 minute (or microwave on HIGH about 4 minutes). Stir in cream and lemon juice.

1 Remove vein from scallops. Combine scallops in saucepan with

2 Melt butter in saucepan (or microwave on HIGH 1 minute), stir in cornflour, stir over heat 1 minute (or

3 Combine extra butter in bowl with breadcrumbs and cheese. Spoon scallops and mushrooms into individual heatproof serving dishes; sprinkle with shallots. Spoon sauce over scallops, sprinkle with breadcrumb mixture, place under heated grill until breadcrumbs are golden brown.
  Serves 6.

CREPES

Cooked crêpes can be frozen, with a sheet of greaseproof paper between each crêpe, for up to 2 months. You need a small heavy-based pan with a base measuring about 15cm for cooking the crêpes. See page 22 for how to season the pan. This recipe is unsuitable to microwave.

¾ cup plain flour
3 eggs, lightly beaten
1 tablespoon oil
1 cup milk

1 Sift flour into bowl, make a well in centre. Add combined eggs, oil and milk to well, slowly whisk liquid into flour until batter is smooth.

2 Strain batter into jug to remove any lumps and to make pouring easier.

3 Heat pan over a medium heat, add a small knob of butter and swirl butter evenly around the pan. Pour 2 to 3 tablespoons of batter from jug into pan, swirl round to cover the base of the pan evenly.

4 When crêpe is lightly browned underneath (lift edge of crêpe with spatula to check) carefully lift crêpe, turn to brown other side. This can be done with a spatula or very carefully with fingertips.

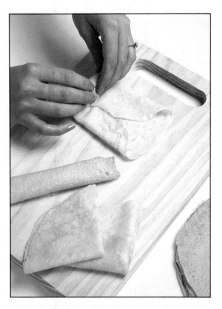

5 There are various ways of folding crêpes for serving. They can be served plain or filled with a variety of fillings. Below are recipes for 2 suitable fillings as well as a recipe for layered crêpes. Each filling is sufficient to fill one quantity of crêpes.
Makes about 12.

SEAFOOD FILLING WITH TOMATO SAUCE

12 cooked crêpes
500g uncooked prawns
1 uncooked lobster tail
250g scallops
60g butter
1 clove garlic, crushed
3 teaspoons lemon juice
½ cup dry white wine
⅔ cup cream
1 tablespoon chopped fresh dill
3 teaspoons cornflour
1 tablespoon water
TOMATO SAUCE
1 tablespoon oil
1 onion, chopped
2 tomatoes, peeled, chopped
400g can pimientos, drained, chopped
½ cup water
1 teaspoon sugar

Shell and devein prawns, remove lobster meat from shell, cut meat into 1cm slices; trim scallops. Heat butter in large frying pan, add garlic and seafood, stir over heat for about 5 minutes or until seafood is tender. Remove seafood from pan, drain on absorbent paper. Add lemon juice, wine, cream, dill and blended cornflour and water to pan, stir over heat until mixture boils and thickens. Add seafood, simmer 1 minute. Place about 2 tablespoons of filling on each crêpe, fold crêpe. Place crêpes in single layer in ovenproof dish, bake covered in moderate oven for about 15 minutes.

Serve with tomato sauce.

Tomato Sauce: Heat oil in large saucepan, add onion, stir over heat until onion is soft. Add tomatoes and remaining ingredients, bring to the boil, reduce heat, simmer covered for about 10 minutes. Blend or process sauce, strain, reheat.

CREAMY CHICKEN AND MUSHROOM FILLING

12 cooked crêpes
30g butter
1 onion, thinly sliced
4 bacon rashers, chopped
250g baby mushrooms
⅔ cup sour cream
2 tablespoons brandy
½ chicken stock cube
2 teaspoons cornflour
½ cup water
2 cups chopped cooked chicken
TOPPING
30g butter
1 cup stale breadcrumbs
2 tablespoons chopped parsley
1 cup grated tasty cheese

Heat butter in frying pan, add onion, bacon and mushrooms, stir over heat until onion is soft. Stir in sour cream, brandy, crumbled stock cube and blended cornflour and water. Stir constantly over heat until mixture boils and thickens, reduce heat, stir in chicken, stir over heat further 1 minute. Place 2 tablespoons of filling on each crêpe, roll up crêpes, place in single layer in ovenproof dish. Sprinkle with topping, bake uncovered in moderate oven for about 15 minutes.

Topping: Melt butter in frying pan, stir in breadcrumbs, stir over heat until breadcrumbs are golden brown, stir in parsley and cheese.

LAYERED HERB CREPES

12 cooked crêpes
¼ cup chopped parsley
2 tablespoons chopped fresh basil
2 tablespoons chopped fresh dill
CHIVE BUTTER
125g soft butter
2 tablespoons chopped fresh chives
2 teaspoons French mustard
½ teaspoon grated lemon rind
LEMON SAUCE
15g butter
1 tablespoon plain flour
1¼ cups hot water
1 chicken stock cube
1 egg yolk
1 tablespoon lemon juice
1 tablespoon chopped parsley

Blend or process half the batter and herbs until smooth. Cook herbed batter and plain batter as described in steps 1 to 4 in crêpe recipe.

Spread one plain crêpe with chive butter, top with a herbed crêpe, continue layering with remaining crêpes and chive butter. Place crêpe stack into ovenproof dish, cover, bake in moderate oven for about 10 minutes (or microwave on HIGH for about 2 minutes). Cut into wedges, serve with lemon sauce.

Chive Butter: Place all ingredients in bowl, mix until well combined.

Lemon Sauce: Melt butter in small saucepan, stir in flour, stir constantly over heat for 1 minute. Gradually stir in water and crumbled stock cube, stir constantly over heat until sauce boils and thickens. Reduce heat, quickly stir in combined egg yolk, lemon juice and parsley, reheat.

CRUDITES WITH MAYONNAISE

Crudités are fresh, raw vegetables served as an entree with sauces for dipping. At right are recipes for a Fresh Herb Mayonnaise and Aioli, a garlic-flavoured mayonnaise. The same method is used for both these recipes, the only difference is that one has garlic, and the other fresh herbs. A selection of vegetables can be used; carrots, peppers, celery, cauliflower or any crisp vegetable of your choice. Cut trimmed vegetables into thin strips, store covered in refrigerator for several hours before serving. Mayonnaise can be made up to 2 days ahead of serving time. Use a light salad oil or a good quality olive oil depending on personal taste. This recipe is not suitable to freeze.

FRESH HERB MAYONNAISE
2 egg yolks
¼ teaspoon salt
1 cup oil
1 tablespoon chopped fresh dill
1 tablespoon chopped parsley
1 tablespoon chopped fresh chives
1 teaspoon French mustard
1 tablespoon lemon juice
AIOLI
2 egg yolks
¼ teaspoon salt
4 cloves garlic, crushed
1 cup oil
1 tablespoon lemon juice

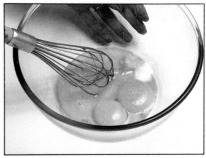

1 Whisk egg yolks, salt and garlic together in bowl until smooth.

2 Gradually whisk in oil drop by drop, whisking constantly until a little over a quarter of the oil has been added. Then, very slowly pour in remaining oil in a thin stream, while whisking constantly. If oil is added too quickly, the mixture will curdle and separate. If this happens, simply place another egg yolk in a clean dry bowl, slowly whisk in the curdled mixture drop by drop, whisking constantly until all the mixture has been added.

3 Add herbs, mustard and lemon juice; mix well.
Makes 1 cup.

Table: Wentworth Antiques; china: Pillivuyt from Hale Imports

The quenelle mixture can be made a day in advance and refrigerated overnight. The cooking must be left to the last minute. The sauce should also be made as close to serving time as possible. This recipe is unsuitable to freeze or microwave.

500g scallops
2 egg whites
½ cup thickened cream
4 green shallots, chopped
1 teaspoon grated lemon rind
SORREL SAUCE
45g butter
1 small leek, chopped
2 cups coarsely chopped sorrel
1 fish stock cube
1 cup water
2 teaspoons plain flour
⅓ cup thickened cream

SCALLOP QUENELLES

1 Remove vein from scallops, wash scallops, drain, pat dry with absorbent paper.

2 Process all ingredients until smooth. Spread evenly onto a flat tray, refrigerate a few hours or overnight until firm.

3 Mould mixture into oval shapes by using 2 wet dessertspoons. Spoon mixture into pan of gently simmering water. Poach for about 3 minutes on each side. It is important not to allow water to come to the boil or quenelles will fall apart.

4 Drain quenelles on absorbent paper while preparing sauce.

Sorrel Sauce: Heat half the butter in a frying pan, add leek, cook, stirring, until leek is soft. Stir in sorrel, reduce heat, cook for 3 minutes. Stir in crumbled stock cube and water, bring to the boil, reduce heat, simmer 3 minutes. Blend or process mixture until smooth. Melt remaining butter in saucepan, stir in flour, cook, stirring constantly, for 1 minute; gradually stir in sorrel mixture. Stir constantly over heat until sauce boils and thickens slightly; stir in cream, reheat before serving.

Serves 6.

GALANTINE OF DUCK

Serve this galantine hot or cold; it will serve more than 6 if sliced thinly when cold. Galantine can be frozen, cooked or uncooked, for up to 2 months; it is unsuitable to microwave.

No. 16 duck
750g chicken mince
2 egg yolks, lightly beaten
2 tablespoons chopped parsley
2 tablespoons tomato paste
1 cup stale breadcrumbs
1 tablespoon currants
500g ham

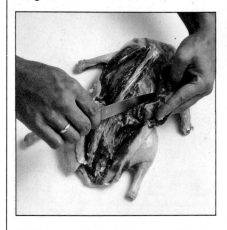

1 Using a sharp knife, cut off wing tips at the second joint. Cut through skin of duck down centre back. Separate flesh from backbone on one side with tip of knife or scalpel. Then, following the shape of the bones, gradually ease flesh away from bones. Repeat process with the other side of the duck.

2 Holding rib cage away from duck, cut breastbone from flesh.

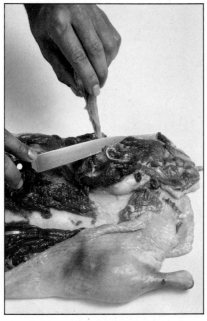

3 Hold up the thigh with one hand, cut around the top of bone to remove flesh, scrape down the bone to next joint, cut around flesh again, scrape down to the end. Pull bone out and cut away. Repeat with other leg bone and both wings. Turn flesh of legs and wings inside duck.

4 Combine chicken mince, egg yolks, parsley, tomato paste, breadcrumbs and currants in a large bowl, mix well. Cut ham into 1cm strips. Spoon half the mixture down centre of duck, top with half the ham, cover with remaining breadcrumb mixture, then remaining ham.

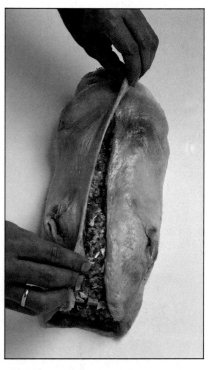

5 Fold one side of duck over breadcrumb mixture, then other side.

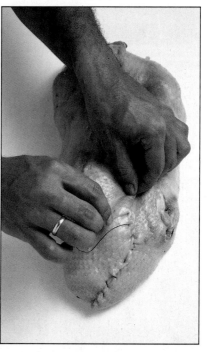

6 Sew duck flesh together using a needle and dark thread. Tie with string at 5cm intervals to keep galantine in shape during cooking. Place galantine in a baking dish, rub with oil. Bake in moderate oven for about 1¼ hours or until duck is tender. Stand 15 minutes, remove string and thread.
Serves 6.

30

Fabric: Les Olivades; platter: Cavendish Blue by Royal Worcester; tankard: from Wentworth Antiques

DUCK
A L'ORANGE

Orange Sauce can be made up to 1 day ahead if desired. This recipe is not suitable to freeze or microwave.

No 20 duck
30g butter, melted
ORANGE SAUCE
1 orange
½ cup orange juice
1 tablespoon sugar
1 tablespoon white vinegar
2 teaspoons lemon juice
2 cups water
1 chicken stock cube
3 teaspoons arrowroot
1 tablespoon water, extra
½ cup Grand Marnier

2 Remove rind from orange, remove any white pith; cut rind into thin strips. Combine rind, orange juice, sugar, vinegar, lemon juice, water and crumbled stock cube in saucepan. Stir over heat until mixture boils, boil rapidly uncovered, without stirring, until mixture is reduced by half.

3 Stir blended arrowroot and extra water gradually into sauce, stir constantly over heat until sauce boils and thickens. Remove from heat, stir in Grand Marnier.

4 Drain pan juices from baking dish, pour sauce over duck, return to oven, bake further 20 minutes, basting frequently with sauce until duck is tender and well glazed.
Serves 4.

1 Tie duck's legs together as shown. Place duck into baking dish, brush duck with butter. Bake in moderate oven for about 1 hour. Brush occasionally with juices during cooking.

This delicious Casserole of Quail on a bed of leeks, mushrooms and ham is best baked just before serving. Quail may be trimmed up to a day ahead and stored covered in the refrigerator. This recipe is unsuitable to freeze or microwave.

6 quail
60g butter
2 leeks, chopped
250g mushrooms, chopped
125g ham, chopped
½ teaspoon dried oregano leaves
½ cup dry white wine
2 tablespoons lemon juice
2 teaspoons cornflour
½ cup water

CASSEROLE OF QUAIL

1 Wash quail, remove necks. Using a knife or a sharp pair of scissors, cut along both sides of backbone, discard backbone of quail.

2 To flatten quail, run your thumb along breastbone as shown, tuck wings under.

3 Heat butter in frying pan, add leeks, cook, stirring, 1 minute, add mushrooms, ham and oregano, cook, stirring, 2 minutes. Transfer mixture to ovenproof dish.

4 Place quail over leek mixture, pour over combined wine and lemon juice. Bake uncovered in moderate oven for about 45 minutes or until quail are tender. Carefully pour liquid from dish into a small saucepan, add blended cornflour and water, cook, stirring constantly, over heat until mixture boils and thickens, pour over quail just before serving.
Serves 6.

SEASONED ORANGE QUAIL

Quail are quite easy to bone out, especially if you use a scalpel (available from chemists); a small sharp pointed knife is also good. Boning out and seasoning can be done the day before cooking; keep covered in refrigerator. The seasoned uncooked quail can be frozen for up to 2 weeks, thaw overnight in refrigerator before cooking. This recipe is not suitable to microwave.

6 quail
6 pitted prunes
60g butter
½ cup dry white wine
2 teaspoons chopped fresh
    marjoram (or ½ teaspoon dried
    marjoram leaves)
½ teaspoon grated orange rind
⅓ cup orange juice
1 tablespoon plain flour
1 cup water
1 chicken stock cube
½ teaspoon sugar
2 tablespoons Grand Marnier

SEASONING
250g minced veal
125g ham, finely chopped
½ cup chopped walnuts
2 teaspoons chopped fresh rosemary
    (or ½ teaspoon dried rosemary
    leaves)
1 egg, lightly beaten
2 tablespoons chopped fresh chives
1 cup stale breadcrumbs

1 Remove rib cage from quail by carefully cutting bone from flesh; leave wings and legs intact. Divide seasoning between quail; place prunes in the centre of the seasoning.

2 Sew quail together using needle and thread. Combine butter, wine, marjoram, orange rind and juice in a small saucepan; bring to the boil, remove from heat. Place quail in a single layer in a baking dish, pour over wine mixture. Bake in moderate oven for about 45 minutes or until quail are tender. Brush occasionally with pan juices during baking. Remove quail from baking dish, cover, keep warm. Place baking dish over heat, stir in flour; cook 1 minute stirring constantly, stir in water, crumbled stock cube and sugar. Bring to the boil, reduce heat, simmer uncovered until slightly thickened; remove from heat, stir in Grand Marnier.
Seasoning: Combine all ingredients in a large bowl; mix well.
    Serves 6.

This dish can be prepared up to the end of step 3 the day before serving; store covered in refrigerator. This recipe is unsuitable to freeze or microwave.

12 chicken drumsticks
2 carrots
2 sticks celery
4 small zucchini
60g butter
1 cup dry white wine
300ml carton cream
1 tablespoon brandy
2 teaspoons seeded mustard

CHICKEN BALLOTINE

1 To prepare the drumsticks, use a small, sharp knife and scrape the meat away from each end of the bone. Pull meat off the bone; as you do this the meat will turn inside out.

2 With meat still inside out, hold onto the white tendons and scrape the meat away until the tendons are released. Turn meat so that the skin is to the outside.

3 Cut carrots, celery and zucchini into thin straws about 10cm long. Take 3 of each and insert them into the chicken drumsticks.

4 Heat butter in large frying pan, add chicken, fry on all sides until chicken is golden brown. Add wine, bring to the boil, cover, reduce heat, simmer 10 minutes or until chicken is tender. Remove chicken, keep warm. Add cream, brandy and mustard to pan, bring to the boil, reduce heat, simmer uncovered 3 minutes or until reduced and thickened slightly. Pour sauce over chicken before serving.
Serves 6.

Table: Wentworth Antiques;; pan: Copco from Vasa Agencies

2 Cover tomatoes with boiling water, stand 1 minute. Peel off skin; chop tomatoes roughly.

3 Combine tomatoes in pan with mushrooms, onion, garlic, water and crumbled stock cube, wine, brandy, tomato paste and basil. Bring to the boil, reduce heat, simmer covered, 10 minutes (or microwave on HIGH about 5 minutes).

CHICKEN MARENGO

This dish can be made the day before required; store, covered in refrigerator. It can also be frozen in an airtight container for up to 2 months; thaw overnight in refrigerator before reheating.

4 chicken thighs
4 chicken drumsticks
plain flour
30g butter
2 tablespoons oil
3 large ripe tomatoes
250g mushrooms, sliced
1 large onion, chopped
2 cloves garlic, crushed
¾ cup water
1 chicken stock cube
¾ cup dry white wine
2 tablespoons brandy
2 tablespoons tomato paste
1 tablespoon chopped fresh basil
500g cooked prawns, shelled

1 Toss chicken in flour. Heat butter and oil in large saucepan, add chicken, fry until golden brown all over, remove from pan. Drain fat from pan.

4 Return chicken to pan, cover, cook further 30 minutes (or microwave on HIGH about 10 minutes). Remove cover, cook further 20 minutes or until chicken is tender (or microwave on HIGH about 10 minutes). Serve topped with prawns.
Serves 4.

This dish can be made the day before required and kept covered in refrigerator; it is usually served with rice. This recipe is unsuitable to freeze or microwave.

6 chicken breast fillets
30g butter
250g mushrooms, sliced
1 red pepper, chopped
1 green pepper, chopped
60g butter, extra
300ml carton cream
4 egg yolks
1 tablespoon brandy

CHICKEN A LA KING

1 Cut chicken into bite-sized pieces. Remove any fat and sinew.

2 Melt butter in large frying pan, add mushrooms and peppers, fry until peppers are tender, drain on absorbent paper.

3 Melt extra butter in frying pan, add chicken pieces in single layer, fry until chicken is golden brown (do not allow butter to burn). Add cream, stir over heat until chicken is tender.

4 Remove pan from heat, stir in combined egg yolks and brandy; stir in mushrooms and peppers. Return pan to heat, gently reheat mixture, stirring constantly, without boiling.
Serves 4

2 Melt butter in large frying pan, add chicken in single layer, fry until golden brown all over; remove from pan. Drain all but 1 tablespoon of fat from pan.

3 Add bacon, onions and garlic to frying pan, fry until onions are browned. Stir in red wine, water and crumbled stock cube, brandy and tomato paste. Return chicken to pan, bring to the boil, cover, reduce heat, simmer 30 minutes (or microwave on HIGH about 15 minutes).

4 Add mushrooms, simmer uncovered further 10 minutes or until chicken is tender (or microwave on HIGH about 10 minutes). Remove chicken to serving plate. Stir blended flour and water into pan, stir constantly over heat until mixture boils and thickens, stir over heat for 1 minute (or microwave on HIGH about 3 minutes), pour sauce over chicken.
Serves 4.

COQ AU VIN

The flavour will improve if this dish is made the day before required. This recipe is unsuitable to freeze.

No. 15 chicken
60g butter
4 bacon rashers, chopped
375g (about 16) baby onions
2 cloves garlic, crushed
1½ cups dry red wine
1 cup water
1 chicken stock cube
2 tablespoons brandy
1 tablespoon tomato paste
250g baby mushrooms
1 tablespoon plain flour
2 tablespoons water

1 Cut chicken into serving-sized pieces; remove any fat.

Both sauces make sufficient quantity for 6 chicken fillets, they need to be made as close to serving time as possible. The grapes for sauce veronique can be peeled and refrigerated the day before required. Use a sharp knife or fingernails to peel away the skin; we didn't discover an easier way. These sauces are not suitable to freeze or microwave.

6 chicken breast fillets
1 tablespoon oil
30g butter
Heat oil and butter in a large frying pan, add chicken in a single layer, cook over fairly high heat until chicken is lightly browned and tender; this will take about 10 minutes, depending on size and thickness of the fillets. Overcooking dries out these fillets. Serve chicken with the sauce of your choice.

SAUCE VERONIQUE
1 cup dry white wine
1½ cups water
¼ cup dry vermouth
30g butter
¼ cup cream
½ cup small white seedless grapes, peeled
2 teaspoons cornflour
1 tablespoon water

1 Combine wine, water and vermouth in a medium saucepan, bring to the boil, boil rapidly until reduced by half. Reduce heat, stir in butter, cream and grapes, stir over heat without boiling until the butter is melted.

2 Stir in blended cornflour and water, stir constantly over heat until mixture boils and thickens.

CHICKEN WITH TWO SAUCES

FRESH TARRAGON SAUCE
30g butter
1 clove garlic, crushed
2 tablespoons chopped fresh tarragon
1 teaspoon French mustard
1 teaspoon lemon juice
⅓ cup brandy
½ cup cream

1 Heat butter and garlic in small saucepan. Add combined tarragon,

mustard, lemon juice and brandy. Bring to the boil, reduce heat, simmer uncovered 2 minutes.

2 Gradually stir in cream, reheat without boiling.

CHICKEN CHAUD-FROID

This recipe can be prepared a day ahead of serving. It is unsuitable to freeze or microwave.

1 litre (4 cups) water
2 chicken stock cubes
1 stick celery, chopped
1 teaspoon whole black peppercorns
1 bay leaf
6 chicken breasts
SAUCE
2 teaspoons gelatine
1 cup mayonnaise
1 tablespoon lemon juice
300ml carton thickened cream
ASPIC JELLY
1 cup water
¼ cup dry sherry
1 tablespoon gelatine

bay leaf in a large deep frying pan, bring to the boil, gradually add chicken to pan in single layer; bring to boil, reduce heat, simmer covered for about 8 minutes or until chicken is just tender.

2 Remove chicken from pan, drain on wire rack over a tray, cool to room temperature, refrigerate chicken covered for about 15 minutes. Strain cooking liquid through fine sieve; reserve 1 cup stock for sauce.

3 Coat chicken evenly with sauce, refrigerate for about 5 minutes; repeat process about 3 times or until chicken is evenly coated all over. Serve on chopped aspic.

Sauce: Sprinkle gelatine over the cup of reserved stock, dissolve over hot water; cool without setting, stir in remaining ingredients.

Aspic Jelly: Combine water, sherry and gelatine in bowl, stir until dissolved over pan of hot water. Pour into Swiss roll pan; refrigerate until set before cutting into diamond shapes.

Serves 6.

1 Combine water, crumbled stock cubes, celery, peppercorns and

Table: Freedom Furniture; platter: by Strachan from R. P. Symonds; glass: Studio Haus

There are many variations of this classic recipe, ours is made rich and delicious with the addition of port and red wine. Any good stewing steak is ideal for this recipe. It is best made a day or so before serving to enhance and develop flavours. When flaming dishes it is necessary to have the alcohol warm before igniting it with a match (or taper for safety). Be sure any exhaust fan over the cooking top is off before flaming any alcohol. This recipe can be frozen for up to 2 months but is unsuitable to microwave.

1½kg rib steak
60g butter
2 tablespoons brandy
250g baby mushrooms
200g baby onions
30g butter, extra
2 cups dry red wine
1 cup port
1 cup water
½ cup canned tomato puree
2 bay leaves
2 tablespoons cornflour

BOEUF BOURGUIGNONNE

1 Cut steak into large cubes. Heat butter in a large frying pan, add steak to pan in small quantities, cook stirring, over heat until well browned all over. This will give the dish a good rich colour. Remove steak as it is browned. Return steak to the pan with the brandy, flame the brandy, when the flame has subsided, remove steak.

2 Remove stalks from mushrooms, remove outer skins from onions, add whole mushrooms and onions to pan with extra butter, cook, stirring, 2 minutes, remove mushrooms and onions from pan.

3 Return steak to pan, add wine, port, half the water, tomato puree and bay leaves. Bring to the boil, re-duce heat, cover, simmer 1 hour or until steak is tender.

4 Add mushrooms and onions to pan, cook uncovered 30 minutes. Stir in blended cornflour and remaining water, stir constantly over heat until mixture boils and thickens.
Serves 6.

Bowl: Manoir from Villeroy & Boch

41

BEEF PAUPIETTES

Paupiettes can be prepared and rolled, then frozen for up to a month, or can be prepared a day before cooking and serving; keep refrigerated. This recipe is unsuitable to microwave. Cassis is a blackcurrant-flavoured liqueur.

6 beef eye-fillet steaks
125g lamb mince
1 red pepper, finely chopped
1 cup stale breadcrumbs
2 bacon rashers, finely chopped
2 tablespoons chopped fresh chives
1 tablespoon chopped fresh mint
1 egg, lightly beaten
plain flour
90g butter
2 tablespoons oil
CASSIS SAUCE
1 tablespoon plain flour
2 tablespoons Cassis
1 cup water
1 beef stock cube

2 Cover steaks with plastic wrap; pound until thin.

1 Using a sharp knife, cut steaks in half crossways.

3 Combine mince, pepper, breadcrumbs, bacon, chives, mint and

egg in a large bowl; mix well. Place about 2 tablespoons of lamb mixture onto each steak.

4 Roll steaks, secure with toothpicks, toss rolls in flour. Heat butter and oil in large frying pan, gradually add rolls in single layer, cook for about 10 minutes turning constantly or until rolls are browned and tender. Drain on absorbent paper; serve with sauce.

Cassis Sauce: Drain fat from frying pan except for 1 tablespoon of fat, add flour, cook 1 minute stirring constantly. Remove from heat, stir in Cassis, gradually stir in combined water and crumbled stock cube, stir constantly over heat until sauce boils and thickens, reduce heat, simmer uncovered for about 3 minutes.

Serves 6.

Plate: Lifestyle Imports

Use flavoured butters to make delicious toppings for grilled or pan-fried steak, or to top chicken, fish or vegetables. One quantity of each butter is sufficient for 6 steaks. Each butter is prepared following the same steps, they can be prepared up to a week ahead, wrapped in plastic wrap and refrigerated; they can also be frozen for up to 3 months. We pan-fried beef eye-fillet steaks, and topped them with a slice of flavoured butter just before serving.

HORSERADISH BUTTER
125g butter, chopped
1½ tablespoons horseradish relish
1 tablespoon chopped fresh dill
1 teaspoon grated fresh ginger
1 teaspoon sugar

ROQUEFORT BUTTER
125g butter, chopped
100g Roquefort cheese, chopped
1 teaspoon grated lemon rind
1 teaspoon dry mustard

MAITRE D'HOTEL BUTTER
125g butter, chopped
2 teaspoons lemon juice
2 tablespoons chopped parsley
1 tablespoon chopped fresh chives

BUTTERED STEAKS

1 Combine all ingredients in electric mixer or processor, beat or process until combined.

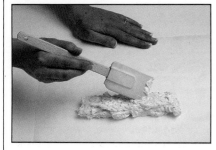

2 Spoon mixture onto a sheet of greaseproof paper in a rough log shape, about 4cm x 15cm.

3 Fold one side of the paper over roll, then, with a ruler, push against the butter as shown, so that the mixture forms a smooth roll. Roll the butter in the greaseproof paper, refrigerate.

4 Remove greaseproof paper from the roll. Cut butter into slices, or use small fancy cutters for different shapes. Refrigerate butter slices until they are required.

1 Heat butter in a large frying pan (or 2 medium frying pans); add steaks in a single layer, cook over high heat for 3 minutes on each side. If medium to well-done steak is preferred, reduce heat and continue to cook steak until it is cooked as desired.

2 Transfer steaks to baking dish, cover, keep warm in a slow oven; discard butter in pan.

3 Add peppercorns and brandy to pan; ignite the brandy, remove from heat, allow flame to subside. Stir in port, mustard and cream; bring to the boil, stir constantly for a few minutes until sauce is slightly thickened; serve over steaks immediately.
Serves 6.

PEPPER STEAK

Steak au poivre is the French name for this popular recipe; there are many variations, this is the one we like best. Remember not to have an exhaust fan on over the stove top when flaming alcohol. This recipe is unsuitable to freeze or microwave.

60g butter
6 beef eye-fillet steaks
1 tablespoon canned drained green peppercorns, crushed
1 tablespoon brandy
2 tablespoons port
1 tablespoon seeded mustard
300ml carton thickened cream

Fabric: Les Olivades; plate: Lorenzo by Mikasa; cutlery: Mikasa

Béarnaise sauce is a perfect accompaniment to steak and roast beef. We pan-fried eye-fillet steaks in about 2 tablespoons of oil. This sauce is enough for 6 thick steaks but it can also be served with steamed vegetables. The most important parts to making this sauce are adding the butter slowly and making sure the mixture does not get too hot. If the sauce does curdle, remove top saucepan immediately from the simmering water, quickly whisk in 1 tablespoon boiling water; this will bring the sauce back to the correct consistency. Continue to whisk in the butter, return to simmering water when saucepan has cooled. Sauce will keep several days covered in the refrigerator. Remove from refrigerator, stand sauce several hours before use to allow it to return to room temperature, stir to reconstitute to sauce consistency. Do not reheat as sauce is inclined to curdle. This recipe is not suitable to freeze or microwave.

½ cup white vinegar
3 green shallots, chopped
8 whole black peppercorns
1 bay leaf
¼ teaspoon dried tarragon leaves
4 egg yolks
250g butter

BEARNAISE SAUCE

1 Combine vinegar, shallots, peppercorns, bay leaf and tarragon in small saucepan, bring to the boil, reduce heat, simmer uncovered until mixture is reduced by half. Strain, reserve liquid.

2 Place egg yolks in top half of double saucepan, stir until combined. Gradually stir in reserved liquid. Cut butter into small cubes.

3 Place top of double saucepan in position over barely simmering

water. Simmering water should not touch the base of the top saucepan. Gradually whisk in the butter a cube at a time. Do not allow water in bottom saucepan to boil. If top saucepan becomes very hot, remove from simmering water, continue to whisk in butter gradually off the heat. When saucepan has cooled slightly, return to position over simmering water, whisk in remaining butter gradually.

4 Once all the butter has been added, the mixture should have thickened to the consistency shown. Remove from water immediately, pour into serving jug, stand covered ready to serve.

BEEF PROVENCALE

This recipe can be made the day before required; it is unsuitable to freeze.

1kg oyster blade steak
60g butter
2 leeks, sliced
2 cloves garlic, crushed
400g can tomatoes
2 bay leaves
1 tablespoon fresh thyme leaves
   (or 1 teaspoon dried thyme leaves)
1 cup water
1 beef stock cube
1½ cups dry red wine
500g baby potatoes
4 small zucchini, sliced
12 black olives
1 tablespoon plain flour
2 tablespoons water

2 Add leeks and garlic to pan, fry until leeks are lightly browned.

3 Stir in undrained crushed tomatoes, bay leaves, thyme, water and crumbled stock cube, wine, potatoes and steak. Bring to the boil, reduce heat, cover, simmer 40 minutes or until steak is tender (or transfer mixture to shallow ovenproof dish, cover, microwave on HIGH for about 20 minutes).

1 Cut fat and sinew from steak. Cut steak into bite-sized pieces. Melt butter in large saucepan, add steak in single layer, fry until well browned all over; remove from pan.

4 Add zucchini and olives, cook further 10 minutes (or microwave on HIGH about 8 minutes). Blend flour with water, stir into mixture, stir over heat until mixture boils and thickens (or microwave on HIGH 3 minutes).
Serves 4.

Table: Wentworth Antiques; china: Corso di Fiori.

1kg beef eye fillet
30g butter, melted
1 tablespoon oil
1 clove garlic, crushed
2 teaspoons coarsely ground black
   pepper
SAUCE BORDELAISE
1½ cups water
2 beef stock cubes
1 cup dry red wine
2 tablespoons tomato paste
2 green shallots, chopped
1 sprig parsley
1 bay leaf
2 teaspoons plain flour
60g butter

1 Trim fillet, tie with string to keep a good shape during cooking. Place fillet on a rack in a baking dish, brush with combined butter, oil and garlic. Sprinkle with pepper, bake in hot oven for 10 minutes, reduce heat to moderate, cook further 20 minutes or until beef is cooked to your taste.

BEEF BORDELAISE

We used a whole piece of beef eye fillet; it is enough to serve 6 people. The fillet is best roasted just before serving time. This recipe is unsuitable to freeze or microwave.

2 **Sauce Bordelaise:** Combine water, crumbled stock cubes, wine, tomato paste, shallots, parsley and bay leaf in small saucepan, bring to the boil, reduce heat, simmer until mixture is reduced to about 1 cup liquid, strain, discard shallot mixture.

3 Pour any pan drippings from beef into small frying pan, add flour, cook, stirring, until brown, gradually add wine mixture. Bring to the boil stirring constantly, reduce heat, simmer uncovered for a few minutes. Gradually whisk in small pieces of cold butter over heat, whisk well after each addition. Serve immediately.
   Serves 6.

VEAL RAGOUT

A ragoût is simply a stew; any cut of veal can be used for this recipe, for example, stewing veal, chops or any cut of steak. Ragoût can be made the day before required. It can be frozen for up to 2 months; thaw in refrigerator before reheating.

1kg nut of veal
30g butter
1 tablespoon oil
1½ tablespoons plain flour
2 cups water
2 beef stock cubes
¼ cup tomato paste
2 cloves garlic, crushed
1 teaspoon dried marjoram leaves
2 carrots, sliced
2 sticks celery, sliced
2 potatoes, quartered
1½ cups (250g) frozen peas

2 Add flour, cook, stirring, for 1 minute. Stir in water and crumbled stock cubes, tomato paste, garlic and marjoram, bring to the boil, cook 1 minute. Return veal to pan, cover, simmer 20 minutes (or transfer mixture to shallow ovenproof dish, cover, microwave on MEDIUM for 15 minutes).

3 Add carrots, celery and potatoes, simmer further 30 minutes or until vegetables are tender (or microwave covered on HIGH about 15 minutes).

1 Remove all fat and sinew from veal, cut veal into bite-sized pieces. Heat butter and oil in large saucepan, add veal in single layer, cook, stirring, until golden brown all over. Remove veal from pan, drain all but 2 tablespoons of fat from pan.

4 Add peas, cook further 5 minutes (or microwave covered on HIGH about 3 minutes).
Serves 4.

Dish: Chambord by Bodum from Vasa Agencies

8 small veal steaks
4 slices ham
4 slices gruyère cheese
plain flour
2 eggs, lightly beaten
¼ cup milk
1 tablespoon grated lemon rind
2 cups packaged breadcrumbs
2 cups stale breadcrumbs
60g butter
¼ cup oil

VEAL CORDON BLEU

Steaks can be filled and crumbed the day before serving; cover loosely, store in refrigerator. This recipe is unsuitable to freeze or microwave.

1 Trim veal of any membrane (this will cause the veal to curl up during cooking if left intact). Use a meat mallet or rolling pin to pound veal thinly, trim edges neatly.

2 Place a slice of ham and cheese over 4 of the steaks; filling should come to within 1cm of the edge of the steaks. Cover with remaining steaks, press edges firmly together.

3 Dust steaks lightly with flour, then dip in combined eggs and milk and lemon rind; coat with combined breadcrumbs, press crumbs on firmly. Refrigerate steaks 1 hour. Heat butter and oil in large frying pan, add steaks, cook over medium heat for about 3 minutes on each side or until golden brown; drain on absorbent paper.

Serves 4.

VEAL OSCAR

This recipe is best prepared just before serving; the sauce will not reheat successfully without curdling. This recipe is unsuitable to freeze or microwave.

½ cup white wine vinegar
3 green shallots, chopped
1 teaspoon whole black peppercorns
1 bay leaf
4 egg yolks
250g butter
2 tablespoons chopped fresh mint
6 veal steaks
plain flour
90g butter, extra
2 tablespoons oil
340g can asparagus spears, drained
1 cooked lobster tail, sliced

1 Combine vinegar, shallots, peppercorns and bay leaf in a small frying pan, bring to the boil, reduce heat, simmer uncovered until mixture is reduced by half; strain, reserve liquid.

2 Melt butter in small saucepan. Process egg yolks until smooth. With

motor operating, gradually add hot bubbling butter then the reserved liquid. Add mint, process 5 seconds.

3 Trim veal, remove any membrane (this will cause veal to "curl" during cooking), cover with plastic wrap, pound thinly. Toss veal in flour. Heat extra butter and oil in large frying pan, add veal in single layer, cook few minutes on both sides until golden brown and tender; drain. Top the veal with asparagus and lobster, serve immediately with sauce.

Serves 6.

Plate: Grandeur Gray from Mikasa

Fricadelles are patties made from minced veal and cream. Uncooked patties and sauces can be frozen for up to 2 months. Fricadelles can be shaped and crumbed the day before serving, covered loosely and stored in the refrigerator. Both sauces may be made up to a day ahead; store covered, reheat. This recipe is unsuitable to microwave.

6 veal steaks
½ cup cream
½ cup stale breadcrumbs
½ teaspoon ground nutmeg
1 egg, lightly beaten
¼ cup milk
1 cup packaged breadcrumbs
½ cup stale breadcrumbs, extra
60g butter
2 tablespoons oil
SOUR CREAM SAUCE
30g butter
1 onion, finely chopped
2 tablespoons white vinegar
2 tablespoons lemon juice
2 teaspoons plain flour
300ml carton thickened cream
TOMATO SAUCE
1 tablespoon oil
1 clove garlic, crushed
3 large tomatoes, peeled, chopped

VEAL FRICADELLES

1 Trim veal of any membrane, process or mince veal finely; gradually add cream while processing. Transfer mixture to a large bowl, mix in breadcrumbs and nutmeg.

2 Divide mixture into six equal portions, shape into patties, dip each into combined egg and milk, then toss in combined breadcrumbs; press crumbs on firmly.

3 Heat butter and oil in frying pan, add patties, fry over medium heat for about 5 minutes, turning once during cooking. Drain on absorbent paper, place on oven tray, bake further 15 minutes in moderate oven.

4 **Sour Cream Sauce:** Heat butter in small saucepan; add onion, cook, stirring, until onion is soft, add vinegar and lemon juice, cook 1 minute. Stir in blended flour and cream, cook, stirring, until sauce boils and thickens.
Tomato Sauce: Heat oil and garlic in frying pan, add tomatoes, cook, stirring, until tomatoes are soft.
Makes 6.

2 Combine bacon, shallots and garlic in bowl; mix well. Place spoonfuls of mixture onto each piece of tripe, roll firmly, secure with toothpicks.

3 Heat oil in large saucepan, add onions, carrots and oregano, fry over heat until onions are soft; stir in tomatoes. Place tripe on top of vegetables, add water and crumbled stock cubes. Bring to the boil, reduce heat, cover, simmer 1 hour. Remove cover, simmer further 1 hour or until tripe is tender.

TRIPE AND BACON ROLLS

Honeycomb tripe is best for this recipe. The cooking time advised is only a guide, simply simmer the tripe until it is tender. This recipe may be prepared up to the end of step 3 the day before serving; it is unsuitable to freeze or microwave.

1¼ kg honeycomb tripe
6 bacon rashers, chopped
6 green shallots, chopped
4 cloves garlic, crushed
2 tablespoons oil
3 onions, chopped
3 carrots, chopped
2 teaspoons dried oregano leaves
3 large ripe tomatoes, peeled, chopped
5 cups water
2 chicken stock cubes
1 tablespoon cornflour
¼ cup water, extra

1 Add tripe to large saucepan of cold water, cover, bring to the boil. Reduce heat, simmer covered 1 hour; drain. Cut tripe into 6cm x 8cm pieces.

4 Transfer tripe rolls to serving dish; remove toothpicks. Skim off any fat from the top of the stock. Blend cornflour with extra water, stir into vegetable mixture, bring to the boil, stirring constantly, reduce heat, simmer a few minutes, serve spooned over tripe.
Serves 4.

Screen: John Normyle; remaining props: Appley Hoare Antiques

Brains may be crumbed, covered loosely and stored in refrigerator up to a day before required. Vegetables may be stored covered in refrigerator. Tomato Coulis may be made a day ahead; reheat gently. This recipe is unsuitable to freeze or microwave.

6 sets lambs' brains
1 leek
2 sticks celery
2 zucchini
1 red pepper
1 egg, lightly beaten
¼ cup milk
1½ cups packaged breadcrumbs
30g butter
¼ cup oil
30g butter, extra
1 clove garlic, crushed
TOMATO COULIS
400g can tomatoes
½ teaspoon sugar
1 teaspoon grated lemon rind

WARM SALAD OF BRAINS

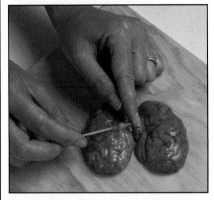

1 Place brains in bowl, cover with cold water, stand 1 hour, drain, peel away membrane. Place brains in pan, cover with cold water, bring to the boil, reduce heat, simmer uncovered 2 minutes, drain on absorbent paper; cool to room temperature.

2 Cut leek, celery, zucchini and pepper into thin 6cm strips.

3 Dip brains into combined egg and milk, coat with breadcrumbs, press crumbs on firmly, refrigerate 1 hour. Heat butter and oil in frying pan, add brains, cook over medium heat on both sides until golden brown, drain on absorbent paper, keep warm.

4 Heat extra butter and garlic in frying pan, add vegetables, cook, stirring, 2 minutes, place vegetables on serving plate, top with brains, serve with tomato coulis.
Tomato Coulis: Blend or process all ingredients until smooth. Strain, heat coulis in saucepan before serving.
  Serves 6.

LAMB'S FRY CASSEROLE

Lamb's liver is called lamb's fry. It is important to remove the membrane from the fry as it toughens on cooking. A short cooking time over a fairly high heat will give you the best results; overcooking dries out the delicate livers. It should be cooked and served immediately for tastiest eating. This recipe is not suitable to freeze or microwave.

750g lamb's fry
90g butter
6 bacon rashers, chopped
1 clove garlic, crushed
2 onions, chopped
1 tablespoon plain flour
2 cups water
2 beef stock cubes
2 tablespoons tomato paste
400g can tomatoes
3 sticks celery, chopped
3 large (500g) parsnips, chopped

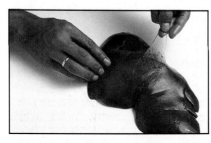

1 Remove membrane from lamb's fry, soak fry in water for 30 minutes.

Drain, pat dry with absorbent paper. Slice fry thinly.

2 Heat butter in large frying pan, add bacon to pan, cook, stirring, until bacon is crisp. Remove bacon from pan, reserve pan drippings. Heat pan drippings, gradually add fry to pan in single layer, cook over high heat until well browned all over; remove from pan, reserve pan drippings.

3 Add garlic and onions to pan, cook, stirring, until onions are soft. Add flour, cook, stirring, for 1 minute, gradually stir in combined water and crumbled stock cubes, stir over heat until mixture boils and thickens.

4 Stir in tomato paste, undrained crushed tomatoes, celery and parsnips. Bring to the boil, reduce heat, simmer uncovered for about 15 minutes or until parsnips are tender. Return lamb's fry and bacon to pan, reheat gently.
Serves 4 to 6.

Victorian glass: Architectural Heritage, Glebe; napkin: Hampshire and Loundes; dish: Barbara's House & Garden

Ask the butcher to tunnel bone the leg of lamb for you. The lamb can be seasoned and baked the day before required, cooled, covered and refrigerated. Allow the lamb to return to room temperature before wrapping in pastry. Pastry can be wrapped around lamb 2 hours before cooking. Buy or make your own favourite pâté for this recipe. This recipe is not suitable to freeze or microwave.

2kg leg lamb
2 tablespoons oil
500g packet ready-rolled puff
    pastry roll
1 egg, lightly beaten
SEASONING
100g pâté
125g mushrooms, thinly sliced
2 tablespoons brandy
1 tablespoon fresh rosemary leaves (or
    1 teaspoon dried rosemary leaves)
2 cups stale breadcrumbs
1 egg, lightly beaten
BRANDY SAUCE
2 tablespoons plain flour
1½ cups water
1 beef stock cube
2 tablespoons brandy
1 tablespoon red currant jelly

LAMB EN CROUTE

1 **Seasoning:** Mash pâté in a bowl with a fork, add remaining ingredients; mix well. Spoon seasoning into cavity of lamb, push seasoning right to the end of the cavity.

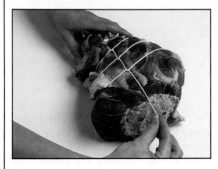

2 Tie lamb with string to keep shape during cooking, place into baking dish. Rub lamb with oil, bake uncovered in moderate oven for 1 hour or until lamb is cooked as desired. Remove lamb, cool to room temperature on wire rack over tray. Reserve 2 tablespoons pan juices for sauce. Pat lamb with absorbent paper; remove string.

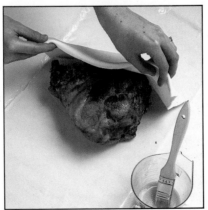

3 Unroll pastry, place lamb upside down in centre, fold one half of pastry over lamb, brush pastry with egg. Fold over other half of pastry, trim away excess pastry, press edges together to enclose lamb completely. Invert lamb so the pastry joins are underneath the lamb.

4 Cut fancy shapes from excess pastry, brush with egg, place on pastry. Place lamb into lightly greased baking dish. Brush pastry all over with remaining egg, bake in a moderately hot oven for about 25 minutes or until pastry is golden brown. Stand lamb 5 minutes before slicing and serve with brandy sauce.

Brandy Sauce: Blend the reserved pan juices in saucepan with the flour, stir constantly over heat until mixture is lightly browned. Gradually stir in water and crumbled stock cube, stir over heat until mixture boils and thickens. Add brandy and red currant jelly, stir over heat until sauce is smooth and heated through.

Serves 6.

China: Manoir by Villeroy & Boch; tiles: Pazotti

55

RACKS OF LAMB

Racks of Lamb are best baked just before serving time. We have given 2 different sauces which will complement the lamb: a rich port sauce flavoured with bacon, the other is mint with lemon. This recipe is not suitable to freeze or microwave.

4 racks of lamb (4 cutlets in each)
ground black pepper
PORT AND ROSEMARY SAUCE
1 onion, chopped
2 bacon rashers, chopped
1 tablespoon chopped fresh
  rosemary (or 1 teaspoon dried
  rosemary leaves)
½ cup port
¼ cup water
½ cup cream
LEMON AND MINT SAUCE
¼ cup lemon juice
¼ cup dry white wine
¼ cup water
1 tablespoon brown sugar
2 teaspoons grated lemon rind
90g unsalted butter
1 tablespoon mint jelly

1 Trim any excess fat from lamb, sprinkle lamb with pepper. Place lamb on a rack in a baking dish. Bake in moderate oven for about 45 minutes or until lamb is cooked as desired. Serve with the sauce of your choice.

2 **Port and Rosemary Sauce:** Pour any pan drippings from lamb into a small frying pan, add onion and bacon, cook, stirring, until bacon is crisp. Add rosemary, port and water, bring to the boil, reduce heat, simmer uncovered until reduced to ½ cup liquid. Add cream, simmer, stirring, until slightly thickened; strain before serving.

3 **Lemon and Mint Sauce:** Combine lemon juice, wine and water in a small frying pan, bring to the boil, reduce heat, simmer uncovered until reduced to ½ cup liquid. Stir in brown sugar and lemon rind, gradually add small pieces of the chopped cold butter over the heat, whisking well after each addition, whisk in mint jelly. Serve immediately.
Serves 4.

China: Howard Black by Royal Worcester; tiles: Pazotti

Noisettes are lamb shortloin chops with the bone removed, the "tail" wrapped around and secured with toothpicks. This dish will improve in flavour if cooked the day before required; keep covered in refrigerator. This recipe is unsuitable to freeze.

1 tablespoon oil
30g butter
6 lamb noisettes
1 onion, chopped
2 cloves garlic, crushed
⅓ cup plain flour
1 litre (4 cups) water
2 chicken stock cubes
⅓ cup dry red wine
2 tablespoons tomato paste
1 large sprig fresh rosemary
2 teaspoons fresh thyme leaves
   (or ½ teaspoon dried thyme leaves)
250g green beans
2 sticks celery
250g baby carrots

NAVARIN OF LAMB

1 Heat oil and butter in frying pan, add noisettes, fry on both sides until browned, remove from pan. Drain all but 2 tablespoons of fat from pan.

2 Add onion and garlic to pan, stir constantly over heat until onion is lightly browned. Add flour, stir constantly over heat until mixture is browned. Stir in water and crumbled stock cubes, wine and tomato paste, stir constantly over heat until mixture boils and thickens. Add rosemary and thyme, reduce heat, simmer 3 minutes.

3 Top and tail beans, cut beans into 5cm lengths. Cut celery into 5cm lengths.

4 Combine noisettes, beans, celery and carrots in large ovenproof dish, top with sauce, cover, bake in moderate oven for about 1½ hours or until lamb is tender (or microwave on MEDIUM for about 30 minutes).
Serves 6.

Dish: Eversham by Royal Worcester; basket: Barbara's House & Garden

2 Melt butter in baking dish, add onions and garlic, fry, stirring constantly, until onions are lightly browned.

3 Stir in thyme, rosemary, undrained crushed tomatoes, tomato puree, water and crumbled stock cube, then add beans.

LAMB BRETONNE

Recipe may be made up to the end of step 3 the day before required. This recipe is unsuitable to freeze or microwave.

375g haricot beans
60g butter
3 onions, sliced
4 cloves garlic, crushed
1 tablespoon fresh thyme leaves
   (or 1 teaspoon dried thyme leaves)
1 large sprig fresh rosemary (or ½
   teaspoon dried rosemary leaves)
400g can tomatoes
425g can tomato puree
2 cups water
1 chicken stock cube
1½kg leg of lamb

1 Soak beans in water overnight; drain. Cook beans in large saucepan of boiling water for about 1 hour or until beans are tender; drain.

4 Place lamb on top of bean mixture, cover, bake in moderate oven for 1 hour. Bake further 1 hour uncovered or until lamb is tender. Stir bean mixture occasionally during cooking. Turn lamb once during cooking.
   Serves 6.

China: Corso di Fiori

This recipe needs last minute cooking to get the best results; it is unsuitable to freeze or microwave.

4 pork fillets
2 apples, peeled, thinly sliced
1 tablespoon finely chopped
    fresh rosemary
2 cups dry white wine
30g butter
1 tablespoon oil
1 cup cream
2 tablespoons red currant jelly
1 teaspoon cornflour
2 teaspoons lemon juice

1 Trim pork fillets. Combine apples, rosemary and wine in saucepan, bring to the boil, reduce heat, simmer covered for a few minutes or until the apples are just tender; drain, reserve the liquid.

PORK WITH APPLE SAUCE

2 Heat butter and oil in frying pan, add pork, cook until pork is lightly browned all over. Add reserved liquid to pan, bring to the boil, reduce heat, simmer covered 10 minutes or until pork is almost cooked. Remove pork from pan.

3 Stir cream and red currant jelly into pan, stir over heat until combined. Stir in blended cornflour and lemon juice, stir constantly over heat until mixture boils and thickens.

4 Cut pork into slices, return to pan with apple; stir gently until heated through. Serve immediately.
   Serves 4.

Fabric: Les Olivades.; plate: Lifestyle Imports.; glass: Maria by Orrefors.

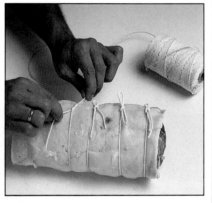

2 Open loin of pork out flat, spread seasoning over centre of pork.

3 Roll pork, tie firmly with string at 5cm intervals.

SEASONED LOIN OF PORK

Ask the butcher to bone out the loin of pork and to leave a long flap to make it easier to season and roll. Pork can be seasoned and frozen for up to a month or refrigerated overnight. It is not suitable to microwave.

2 red peppers, chopped
4 green shallots, chopped
½ cup finely chopped dried apricots
2 egg yolks
2 sticks celery, chopped
2 cups stale breadcrumbs
2½kg loin of pork
PRUNE SAUCE
½ cup finely chopped prunes
½ teaspoon grated lemon rind
2 teaspoons lemon juice
1½ cups water
1 beef stock cube
15g butter
1 tablespoon plain flour

1 Combine peppers, shallots, apricots, egg yolks, celery and breadcrumbs in a large bowl; mix well.

4 Place pork in baking dish, seam side down, bake in hot oven for about 20 minutes or until fat begins to brown. Reduce heat to moderate, bake further 1 hour or until pork is tender; Remove from baking dish, cover, keep warm. Serve with prune sauce.

Prune Sauce: Combine prunes, lemon rind and juice, water and crumbled stock cube in saucepan. Bring to the boil, reduce heat, simmer covered 5 minutes (or microwave on HIGH for about 3 minutes); push through sieve. Drain fat from baking dish. Add butter to baking dish, stir in flour, cook 1 minute, stirring constantly. Remove from heat, gradually stir in prune mixture, stir constantly over heat until sauce boils and thickens, reduce heat, simmer uncovered 3 minutes.

Serves 6 to 8.

Plates: by Limoges from Studio Haus.; glass: Prelude by Orrefors

The pork can be prepared for cooking up to 1 day in advance, stored and covered in refrigerator. Ask your butcher to remove the rind from the pork and to bone it for you, or follow our easy step by step pictures. The cherry sauce must be made just before serving; serve sauce separately as the cherries tend to discolour the pork. This recipe is unsuitable to freeze or microwave.

2½ kg leg of pork
1 onion, sliced
1 tablespoon oil
1 clove garlic, crushed
¼ cup brown sugar
2 x 410g cans black cherries
¼ cup brandy
1 tablespoon lemon juice
2 teaspoons grated lemon rind
1 tablespoon brown sugar, extra
60g butter

PORK WITH CHERRIES

1 Starting at the thick end of the leg of pork, use a sharp knife to cut carefully down and around bone.

2 Scrape away as much meat as possible, remove bone.

3 Cut down (without cutting through) into thickest part of meat, so that meat can be opened out flat.

4 Place onion on a greased sheet of foil. Place pork fat-side up on top of onion; score top of pork, brush with combined oil and garlic. Completely enclose pork in foil. Bake in moderately slow oven for 1 hour. Remove foil, sprinkle pork with sugar, bake pork further 10 minutes in a hot oven or until sugar is melted and golden brown. Stand pork 15 minutes before slicing.

5 Drain cherries, reserve syrup. Combine syrup, brandy, lemon juice, rind and extra sugar in saucepan, bring to the boil, reduce heat, simmer uncovered until reduced by half. Gradually whisk in small pieces of cold butter over heat, whisking well after each addition, add cherries, reheat gently; serve immediately.
Serves 6 to 8.

China: Prelude by Mikasa

61

PORK CASSOULET

Cassoulet can be made the day before required. It can be frozen for up to 2 months; thaw in refrigerator before reheating in a moderate oven for about 30 minutes. This recipe is unsuitable to microwave.

375g lima beans
2 chicken stock cubes
2 cups water
400g can tomatoes
2 tablespoons tomato paste
2 bay leaves
3 cloves garlic, crushed
1 tablespoon fresh thyme leaves (or
    1 teaspoon dried thyme leaves)
2 teaspoons fresh sage leaves (or
    ½ teaspoon dried sage leaves)
30g butter
6 pork medallions
375g thin pork sausages
4 bacon rashers, chopped
3 large onions, chopped

1 Soak beans in water overnight; drain. Cook beans in large saucepan of boiling water for about 1 hour or until beans are tender; drain. Combine beans, crumbled stock cubes, water, undrained crushed tomatoes, tomato paste, bay leaves, garlic and herbs in saucepan, bring to the boil, cover, reduce heat, simmer 30 minutes.

2 Heat butter in large frying pan, add pork, fry over high heat until browned on both sides; remove from pan. Add sausages to pan, fry until golden brown all over, remove from pan. Drain all but 1 tablespoon of fat from pan. Cut sausages into 3 pieces.

3 Add bacon and onions to pan, fry until onions are tender.

4 Combine pork, sausages, bacon and onions in a large baking dish with bean mixture, cover. Bake in moderate oven for about 1½ hours or until pork is tender; stir occasionally.
    Serves 6.

Tiles: Pazotti. Platter: Corso di Fiori

If fresh lemon thyme is unavailable use thyme or parsley. This recipe is unsuitable to freeze or microwave.

3kg fresh mussels
4 green shallots, chopped
1 stick celery, chopped
2 teaspoons chopped fresh lemon
    thyme
2 cups water
½ cup dry white wine
90g butter
2 tablespoons plain flour
300ml carton thickened cream
2 teaspoons sugar
1 tablespoon chopped fresh dill

1 Remove beards from mussels; scrub shells.

MUSSELS IN WHITE WINE

2 Combine mussels, shallots, celery, thyme, water and wine in a large boiler. Bring to the boil, reduce heat, simmer covered for about 5 minutes or until shells have opened; discard any unopened mussels.

3 Strain and reserve cooking liquid. Discard top shell of each mussel. Place mussels on their shells in serving dish; keep warm.

4 Heat butter in saucepan, add flour, cook 1 minute, stirring constantly. Remove from heat, gradually stir in cooking liquid, stir until smooth. Bring to the boil, stirring constantly, reduce heat, simmer uncovered for few minutes. Stir in cream, sugar and dill; re-heat, serve over mussels.
  Serves 4.

SEAFOOD EN BROCHETTE

Make sauce as close to serving time as possible; it is unsuitable for reheating. Soak wooden skewers in water 1 hour before grilling. This recipe is not suitable to freeze or microwave.

36 uncooked king prawns
750g scallops
12 bacon rashers
30g butter, melted
2 teaspoons lemon juice
1 clove garlic, crushed
MOUSSELINE SAUCE
⅓ cup white vinegar
4 whole black peppercorns
1 bay leaf
3 egg yolks
185g butter, melted
½ cup thickened cream

1 Shell and devein prawns, leaving tails intact, devein scallops. Cut bacon into 8cm lengths. Wrap bacon around scallops, thread scallops and prawns alternately onto skewers.

2 Brush the seafood with combined butter, lemon juice and garlic. Grill or barbecue until prawns are cooked and bacon crisp.

3 **Mousseline Sauce.** Combine the vinegar, peppercorns and bay leaf in saucepan, bring to the boil, boil rapidly uncovered until reduced by half, strain, discard peppercorns and bay leaf. Blend or process egg yolks until combined, add half the hot bubbling butter gradually while motor is operating and mixture begins to thicken. Add cooled vinegar mixture gradually. Gradually add remaining butter to processor, continue processing until the mixture is thick.

4 Pour sauce into a bowl, carefully fold in whipped cream. Serve grilled brochettes with boiled rice and mousseline sauce.
Serves 6.

China: Nautilus Collection from Wedgwood

Be careful not to overheat the lobster as it will toughen. This recipe is unsuitable to freeze or microwave.

2 cooked lobsters
1 cup milk
1 small onion, thinly sliced
1 bay leaf
30g butter
2 tablespoons plain flour
300ml carton cream
¾ cup grated tasty cheese
2 teaspoons French mustard
30g butter, extra
4 green shallots, finely chopped
½ cup dry white wine
2 tablespoons grated parmesan
    cheese
1 tablespoon chopped parsley

1 Place lobster on board, insert tip of large sharp knife between eyes, cut in half lengthwise. Remove and discard the greenish grey stomach sac, also the dark vein running the length of the tail. A female lobster will have some red "coral" along the outer side of the white tail meat; this is the roe or eggs. It can be used in sauces or as a garnish. The yellow-brown liquid in the body of the lobster is called the "mustard" and can be incorporated into sauces as well if desired.

Remove tail meat in 1 piece, chop into bite-sized pieces. Remove as much meat as possible from body and claws with skewer or fork, reserve with tail meat for sauce. Rinse shell under cold water; dry well.

LOBSTER THERMIDOR

milk, stir constantly over heat until mixture boils and thickens. Remove mixture from heat, stir in the cream, cheese and mustard.

2 Combine milk, onion, and bay leaf in saucepan, bring to the boil, strain, discard onion and bay leaf. Melt butter in saucepan, stir in flour, stir over heat 1 minute. Gradually stir in hot

3 Melt extra butter in frying pan, add shallots, stir over heat 1 minute, stir in wine, bring to the boil, boil rapidly until quantity is reduced by half. Stir in white sauce mixture and lobster, heat through gently, stirring constantly.

4 Spoon mixture into lobster shells, sprinkle with combined parmesan cheese and parsley. Place under hot griller, grill until cheese is melted and lightly browned.
    Serves 4.

Platter and champagne opener: by Strachan from R. P. Symonds: linen: The Bay Tree

2 Heat butter in saucepan, add flour, cook, stirring constantly, for 1 minute, gradually add milk, stir constantly over heat until the mixture boils and thickens. Reduce heat, add cream and cheese, continue stirring 1 minute, stir in anchovies, add fish.

3 Place half the spinach over bases of greased ovenproof dishes, divide fish mixture evenly amongst dishes. Top with remaining spinach.

FISH FLORENTINE

Fish Florentine may be made up to the stage of baking several hours ahead. We used English spinach, but silver beet may be substituted. We used 6 (1 cup capacity) ovenproof dishes but a large ovenproof dish may be used instead. This recipe is unsuitable to freeze or microwave.

750g white fish fillets
½ cup dry white wine
2 bunches English spinach
30g butter
1 tablespoon plain flour
1 cup milk
½ cup cream
1 cup grated tasty cheese
2 drained canned anchovy fillets, finely chopped
½ cup packaged breadcrumbs
½ cup stale breadcrumbs
½ cup grated tasty cheese, extra

1 Place fish and wine in frying pan, cook over a low heat for about 10 minutes or until fish is just tender. Drain, flake fish, remove any bones. Boil, steam or microwave spinach until just tender.

4 Sprinkle with combined crumbs and extra cheese. Bake in moderate oven for about 30 minutes or until lightly browned.
Serves 6.

Table: Appley Hoare Antiques; basket, broom, napkin: Barbara's House & Garden; dishes: Vasa Agencies

SOLE BONNE FEMME

Our easy to follow steps show you how to skin and trim the whole sole. Sole is best cooked just before serving. This recipe is unsuitable to freeze.

2 whole sole
¼ cup dry vermouth
60g butter
100g baby mushrooms
¼ cup lemon juice
¼ cup dry white wine
2 tablespoons cream
3 green shallots, finely chopped

1 Using your thumb dipped in salt, rub a small amount of salt on the tail of the fish, gradually lifting skin from fish. Carefully peel skin away from flesh working from tail to the head, trim gills. Rinse fish under cold water, dry with absorbent paper.

2 Place fish in a large greased oven-proof dish, add vermouth and half the chopped butter, cover, bake in moderate oven for about 20 minutes or until tender (or microwave on HIGH about 8 minutes). Place fish onto serving plate, keep warm. Strain and reserve cooking liquid.

3 Add remaining butter to frying pan, add mushrooms, cook, stirring, 2 minutes or until mushrooms are lightly browned; remove from pan.

4 Add reserved liquid, lemon juice and wine to pan, cook, stirring, 2 minutes, add cream and shallots, cook, stirring, 1 minute. Serve fish with mushrooms and sauce immediately.
Serves 2.

SEAFOOD PAUPIETTES

Paupiettes can be prepared up to the stage of cooking for up to 6 hours beforehand; keep covered in refrigerator. We used bream fillets in this recipe. This recipe is not suitable to freeze or microwave.

8 thin white fish fillets
PRAWN MOUSSELINE
500g uncooked prawns
1 egg white
¼ cup cream
CURRY SAUCE
30g butter
1 clove garlic, crushed
1 tablespoon plain flour
2 teaspoons curry powder
1 cup water
1 chicken stock cube
¾ cup cream
1 teaspoon lemon juice
2 teaspoons sugar

carefully remove skin from fish, cutting as close as possible to skin.

Prawn Mousseline: Shell and devein prawns. Process prawns, egg white and cream until smooth.

3 Pour enough hot water into oven-proof dish to cover base with about 1cm of water. Cover, bake in moderate oven for about 25 minutes or until rolls are just tender. Prepare sauce while rolls are cooking. Serve paupiettes topped with curry sauce.

Curry Sauce: Melt butter with garlic in saucepan, stir in flour and curry powder, stir constantly over heat for 1 minute. Gradually add water and crumbled stock cube, stir constantly over heat until sauce boils and thickens. Add cream, lemon juice and sugar to sauce, reheat, serve.

Serves 4.

1 Place fish fillets skin-side down on board. Using a thin, sharp knife,

2 Spread each fillet with prawn mousseline. Roll up fillets from the narrow end, secure with toothpicks, place upright in ovenproof dish.

China: Rhodes by Royal Doulton; linen: Jeffcoat Stevenson; caneware: Barbara's House & Garden

The fish and vegetables can be prepared the day before cooking. The sauce must be made and served immediately. This recipe is unsuitable to freeze or microwave.

3 large white fish steaks
1 stick celery
1 carrot
2 tablespoons dry white wine
2 tablespoons white vinegar
2 green shallots, chopped
250g butter
freshly ground black pepper

1 Remove skin and bones from fish, cut steaks into four; shape into medallions, secure medallions with strips of foil and toothpicks.

2 Cut celery and carrot into thin 5cm strips. Add carrot and celery to a small saucepan of boiling water, bring to the boil, reduce heat; simmer 1 minute; drain, rinse vegetables under cold water; drain.

FISH WITH BEURRE BLANC

3 Combine wine, vinegar and shallots in a small saucepan; bring to the boil, reduce heat, simmer uncovered for about 10 minutes or until about a tablespoon of the liquid is left. Whisk in cold chopped butter a few pieces at a time; continue whisking and adding butter over the heat until all the butter is used. Sprinkle fish with black pepper; place fish in a single layer in a baking dish, add enough hot water to come half way up the sides of the fish medallions. Cover dish, bake in moderate oven for about 15 minutes or until the fish is tender. Top fish with vegetables and sauce, serve immediately.

Serves 6.

SNOW EGGS

Snow Eggs can be poached and custard made several hours ahead of serving time, then reheated gently. Toffee is best made just before serving. This recipe is unsuitable to freeze or microwave.

3 eggs, separated
½ cup castor sugar
2½ cups milk
¼ cup castor sugar, extra
½ cup cream
TOFFEE
¼ cup castor sugar
¼ cup light corn syrup

1 Beat egg whites in small bowl with electric mixer until soft peaks form, gradually add sugar a tablespoon at a time, beating well after each addition. Place milk in a frying pan, bring to the boil, reduce heat until milk is barely simmering. Mould meringue mixture into egg shapes using a dessertspoon and spatula. Carefully slide shapes into simmering milk. Poach on one side for about 1 minute, gently turning with slotted spoon, poach another minute. Remove carefully to drain on absorbent paper.

2 Strain milk to remove any egg white. Beat egg yolks and extra sugar in small bowl with electric mixer until thick and creamy, gradually beat in cream. Combine egg mixture and milk in saucepan, cook, stirring constantly over low heat until egg mixture coats the back of a spoon; do not boil or custard will curdle. Place warm custard into serving plates, top with snow eggs, spin toffee strands over snow eggs.

3 **Toffee:** Combine sugar and corn syrup in a saucepan, stir constantly over heat without boiling until sugar is dissolved. Boil rapidly uncovered without stirring for about 5 minutes, or until mixture turns a light golden brown. Remove from heat, allow bubbles to subside, stand 1 minute. Dip two forks, back to back, into toffee mixture and pull toffee into thin strands.
Serves 6.

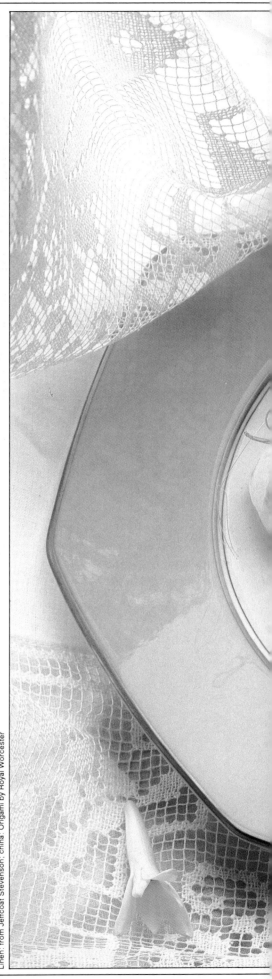

Linen: from Jeffcoat Stevenson; china: Origami by Royal Worcester

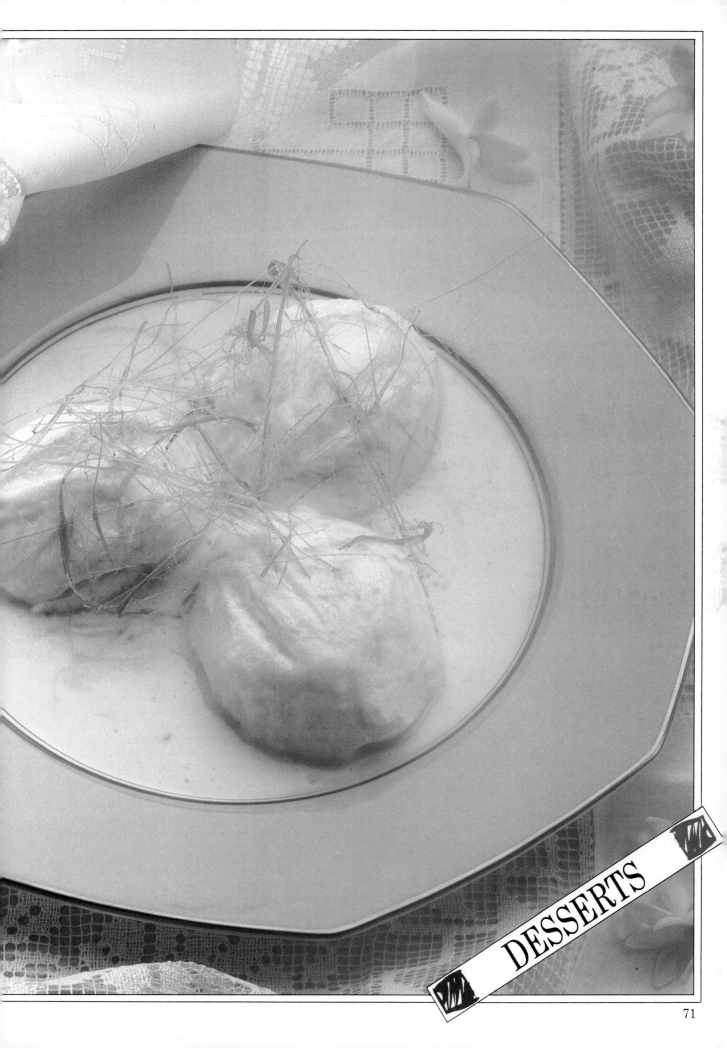

DESSERTS

CHARLOTTE

Charlotte moulds are available from specialty cookware shops. This recipe is best made a day ahead of serving; it is not suitable to freeze or microwave.

90g butter
½ cup milk
2 eggs
1 teaspoon vanilla essence
⅔ cup castor sugar
1 cup self-raising flour
ORANGE SYRUP
½ cup water
¼ cup orange juice
⅓ cup sugar
FILLING
4 egg yolks
2 cups milk
⅔ cup sugar
2 tablespoons plain flour
2 tablespoons cornflour
2 tablespoons Cointreau
½ cup chopped glacé pineapple
¼ cup chopped glacé cherries
½ cup chopped glacé apricots
3 teaspoons gelatine
2 tablespoons water

1 Grease charlotte mould, line base with paper; grease paper. Combine butter and milk in a small saucepan, stir over heat until butter is melted; cool to room temperature.

2 Beat eggs and essence in small bowl with electric mixer until thick and creamy, gradually add sugar, beat until sugar is dissolved. Transfer mixture to large bowl. Lightly fold in half the sifted flour and milk mixture, then remaining flour and milk mixture. Pour into prepared mould, bake in moderate oven for about 45 minutes. Turn onto wire rack to cool.

3 Return sponge to charlotte mould. Cut out inside of sponge, leaving about a 2cm crust. Brush inside of sponge with orange syrup, spoon filling into centre, refrigerate for several hours or overnight. Invert sponge onto a serving plate, decorate with extra whipped cream and maraschino cherries if desired.

Orange Syrup: Combine water, orange juice and sugar in a small saucepan, stir over heat without boiling until sugar is dissolved. Bring to the boil, reduce heat, simmer uncovered without stirring for 3 minutes.

Filling: Blend egg yolks, ¼ cup of the milk, sugar, flour and cornflour in large saucepan, gradually stir in remaining milk. Stir constantly over heat until mixture boils and thickens; stir in Cointreau, then fruit. Add gelatine to water, dissolve over hot water, stir into fruit mixture; cover, cool.

Table: Freedom Furniture; china: Royal Copenhagen from George Jensen; cutlery: George Jensen

Linen: Jeffcoat Stevenson

CARAMEL
¾ cup sugar
¾ cup water
CUSTARD
6 eggs
2 teaspoons vanilla essence
⅓ cup castor sugar
1¾ cups milk
300ml carton thickened cream

CREME CARAMEL

Crème Caramel is perfect made a day before serving. It can be made in individual serving dishes; 1 cup capacity dishes will take about 30 minutes to cook. This recipe is not suitable to freeze or microwave.

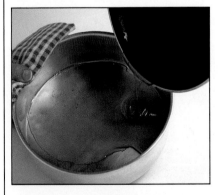

1 Caramel: Combine sugar and water in medium heavy-based saucepan, stir constantly over heat without boiling until sugar is dissolved. Bring to the boil, boil rapidly without stirring for about 5 minutes or until mixture turns golden brown. Pour into deep 20cm round cake pan. Hold the pan with a cloth and quickly tilt pan to coat base evenly. It is correct that the caramel sets at this stage.

2 Custard: Lightly whisk eggs, essence and sugar together in bowl. Combine milk and cream in pan, bring to the boil, allow bubbles to subside from edge of pan. Gradually whisk into egg mixture. Pour custard through a fine strainer over the caramel to remove any tiny specks of egg.

3 Place pan in baking dish with enough boiling water to come halfway up side of pan. Bake in moderately slow oven for about 40 minutes or until custard is just set; it will set more on cooling. Remove from water, stand several hours to cool to room temperature before refrigerating overnight. This method will ensure the caramel will coat the custard when it is turned out. Turn onto serving dish, serve with whipped cream.

1 Grease a deep 23cm round cake pan, line base with paper; grease paper. Melt butter and chocolate in heatproof bowl over hot water; cool to room temperature.

Beat egg yolks, essences and sugar in small bowl with electric mixer until pale and thick. Transfer mixture to large bowl, stir in rum and chocolate mixture, then almonds and sifted flour and cocoa.

2 Beat egg whites in small bowl until soft peaks form, gradually add extra sugar, beat until dissolved between each addition, fold into chocolate mixture. Spread into prepared pan, bake in moderate oven for about 30 minutes. Stand 5 minutes before turning onto wire rack, leave cake upside down.

3 **Glaze:** Combine corn syrup, butter and water in saucepan, stir over heat until mixture comes to the boil; remove from heat. Stir in chocolate, stir until smooth. Stand until bubbles subside, strain, spoon warm glaze over cold cake. Stand at room temperature until set.

CHOCOLATE FUDGE CAKE

Cake can be stored in an airtight container for up to 2 days. Unglazed cake can be frozen for up to 2 months; thaw at room temperature before glazing. This recipe is not suitable to microwave.

90g unsalted butter
90g dark chocolate, chopped
4 eggs, separated
2 teaspoons vanilla essence
¼ teaspoon almond essence
⅔ cup castor sugar
2 tablespoons rum
½ cup packaged ground almonds
½ cup plain flour
½ cup cocoa
¼ cup castor sugar, extra
GLAZE
⅓ cup light corn syrup
30g unsalted butter
2 tablespoons water
100g dark chocolate, chopped

China: Jack Lener Larsen New Spirit by Mikasa

Marquise can be prepared up to the stage of assembling a day ahead. Assemble up to 2 hours before serving. This recipe is unsuitable to freeze.

5 eggs, separated
½ cup castor sugar
1 cup milk
300ml carton thickened cream
1½ tablespoons gelatine
⅓ cup water
¼ cup Grand Marnier
100g dark chocolate, chopped
2 tablespoons slivered almonds
¼ cup sugar

1 Beat egg yolks and sugar in small bowl with electric mixer until pale and thick. Heat milk and half the cream in a saucepan until very hot, gradually add to egg mixture while motor is operating on low speed. Sprinkle gelatine over water, dissolve over hot water, stir into egg mixture.

2 Return mixture to saucepan, stir constantly over low heat without boiling until mixture thickens. Do not boil or mixture will curdle. Transfer mixture to large bowl, cool to luke-warm, stir in Grand Marnier. Beat egg whites in small bowl with electric mixer until soft peaks form; fold into egg mixture in 2 lots. Lightly oil a deep 23cm round cake pan, line base with grease-proof paper, oil paper. Pour mixture into prepared pan, refrigerate until set.

PRALINE MARQUISE

3 Cover base of cake pan or tray with foil. Melt chocolate in bowl over hot water. Spread chocolate smoothly over foil, refrigerate 10 minutes. Cut circles in chocolate with a sharp 4cm cutter, refrigerate until set. Lift circles from foil. Stir almonds constantly in small saucepan over low heat until lightly browned. Spread almonds evenly onto a lightly oiled tray. Place sugar into heavy-based saucepan, cook over medium heat without stirring until sugar starts to melt and brown. Tilt pan over heat until all the sugar is melted and browned. Allow bubbles to subside, pour evenly over almonds. When toffee is set, chop praline finely.

To assemble marquise, turn set custard onto serving plate, press chocolate circles around the side, sprinkle top of custard with praline. Decorate with remaining whipped cream, refrigerate until serving time.

Table: Barbara's House & Garden; china: Ambassador by Crown Derby; bird: Royal Doulton; linen: Jeffcoat Stevenson

2 Cook slowly, loosening edges with knife until crêpe is lightly browned. Turn crêpe with fingers or an egg slide, brown crêpe on other side. Repeat with remaining batter, fold crêpes in half, then in half again.

ALMOND CREPES

These crêpes are made from half flour and half almonds, an unusual variation of the classic French crêpe. Crêpes can be made a day ahead, folded and reheated gently in orange sauce just before serving. Orange sauce can be made several hours ahead. This recipe is unsuitable to freeze or microwave.

½ cup packaged ground almonds
½ cup plain flour
2 eggs, lightly beaten
1 cup milk
125g butter
½ cup castor sugar
1 tablespoon grated orange rind
1 tablespoon grated lemon rind
1 cup orange juice
¼ cup lemon juice
½ cup Grand Marnier
2 oranges

3 Heat butter in a frying pan, add sugar, cook, stirring, over heat until sugar melts and begins to brown. Add combined rinds and juices, stir over high heat until caramelised sugar is dissolved. Add Grand Marnier, bring to the boil, reduce heat, simmer until reduced by about one-third. Place crêpes in sauce, heat through gently.

1 Combine almonds and sifted flour in bowl, gradually stir in eggs and milk, beat until smooth, stand 30 minutes. Heat pan, grease lightly. Pour 2 to 3 tablespoons of batter into pan from a jug, turn pan so batter coats base of pan evenly.

4 Peel rind and pith from oranges. Carefully remove orange flesh between segments as shown. Place crêpes on serving plate, top with orange segments, pour sauce over before serving.
Serves 6.

6 pears
½ cup sauterne
⅓ cup water
MOCHA SAUCE
200g dark chocolate, chopped
300ml carton thickened cream
2 teaspoons instant coffee powder
CARDINALE SAUCE
250g punnet strawberries
250g punnet raspberries
2 tablespoons sugar
2 teaspoons cornflour
1 tablespoon water
1 tablespoon Framboise

POACHED PEARS SAUTERNE

Serve either or both of the sauces with the pears. Each sauce recipe is enough to serve 6 people. Framboise is a raspberry-flavoured liqueur. If pears are to be served cold, they can be poached a day ahead of serving time. This recipe is not suitable to freeze. Sauterne is a sweet dessert wine.

1 Peel pears, trim base so pears will stand upright, place pears in a large saucepan. Pour sauterne and water over the pears, bring to the boil; cover, reduce heat, simmer for 20 minutes or until pears are just tender (or microwave on HIGH for about 10 minutes). Serve pears hot or cold with sauce.

2 **Mocha Sauce:** Combine chocolate, cream and coffee in a saucepan, stir constantly over low heat without boiling until smooth (or microwave on HIGH about 2 minutes).

3 **Cardinale Sauce:** Puree strawberries and raspberries in blender or processor until smooth; strain. Pour into a saucepan, stir in sugar and blended cornflour and water, stir constantly over heat until mixture boils and thickens (or microwave on HIGH for about 3 minutes). Remove from heat, stir in Framboise.
Serves 6.

SORBET IN BRANDY SNAP BASKETS

Sorbets can be made a week in advance; keep covered in freezer. Baskets are best made on the day required as they tend to soften. Framboise is a raspberry-flavoured liqueur. The baskets are not suitable to freeze or microwave.

PLUM SORBET
⅓ **cup sugar**
⅓ **cup water**
425g can plums, drained
2 teaspoons lemon juice
1 tablespoon Framboise
1 egg white
LEMON SORBET
½ **cup sugar**
½ **cup water**
½ **cup dry white wine**
½ **cup lemon juice**
1 egg white
BRANDY SNAP BASKETS
3 tablespoons golden syrup
90g butter
⅓ **cup brown sugar**
½ **cup plain flour**
2 teaspoons ground ginger

1 **Plum Sorbet:** Combine sugar and water in saucepan, stir constantly over heat until sugar is dissolved. Bring to the boil, reduce heat, simmer uncovered without stirring for about 4 minutes or until sugar syrup is thick; cool to room temperature; refrigerate until cold. Combine pitted plums, lemon juice, Framboise and cold syrup in processor, process until smooth. Pour mixture into shallow pan, cover, freeze until firm.

Lemon Sorbet: Combine sugar, water and wine in saucepan, stir constantly over heat until sugar is dissolved. Bring to the boil, reduce heat, simmer uncovered without stirring for about 4 minutes or until syrup is thick. Cool to room temperature, refrigerate until cold. Stir lemon juice into cold syrup, pour into shallow pan, cover, freeze until firm.

2 **Plum Sorbet:** Process frozen plum mixture and egg white until smooth. Return mixture to pan, cover and freeze.
Lemon Sorbet: Process frozen lemon mixture and egg white until smooth. Return mixture to pan, cover, freeze.

3 **Brandy Snap Baskets:** Combine golden syrup, butter and sugar in saucepan, stir constantly over heat without boiling until butter is melted. Remove from heat, stir in sifted flour and ginger.

4 Drop 2 heaped teaspoonfuls of mixture onto lightly greased oven tray. For easy handling, bake only 2 brandy snaps at a time. Bake in moderate oven for about 5 minutes or until golden brown.

5 Stand brandy snaps on tray for about 1 minute or until almost set, lift carefully from tray with spatula.

6 Immediately place brandy snaps over small moulds. While brandy snaps are still pliable, mould with hands into basket shapes, cool on moulds. Continue to make baskets with remaining mixture. Fill baskets with sorbets just before serving.
Serves 8.

78

Large plate: Howard by Royal Worcester; small plate: Morning Lily by Royal Worcester

LIME SABAYON

This fluffy dessert must be made then served immediately; the mixture will separate on standing. Serve with bought biscuits or Almond Tuiles (page 120) or Cats' Tongues (page 122). Sauterne is a dessert wine. This recipe is not suitable to freeze or microwave.

6 egg yolks
¼ cup castor sugar
2 tablespoons sauterne
¼ cup water
1 tablespoon lime juice
1 tablespoon brandy

Combine egg yolks, sugar, sauterne, water and lime juice in top of double saucepan or bowl, place over simmering water; whisk constantly (or beat with rotary beater or electric mixer) for about 10 minutes or until mixture thickens. Do not have the water in the bottom saucepan touching the base of the top saucepan or bowl. Remove from heat, whisk in brandy. Pour into serving glasses. Serve immediately.
Serves 6.

Glasses: Studio Haus; china: Arco Weiss by Villeroy & Boch; linen: Balmain Linen and Lace

4 eggs
½ cup castor sugar
250g can chestnut spread
½ cup self-raising flour
1 tablespoon brandy
150g dark chocolate, chopped
2 x 300ml cartons thickened cream
TOFFEE
1 cup sugar
½ cup water

1 Grease 2 deep 23cm round cake pans, line bases with greaseproof paper; grease paper. Beat eggs in medium bowl with electric mixer until thick and creamy, gradually add sugar, beat until dissolved between each addition. Add ½ cup of the chestnut spread, beat until combined. Fold in sifted flour and brandy. Pour mixture into prepared pans. Bake in moderate oven for about 20 minutes. Turn onto wire rack to cool. Melt chocolate in heatproof bowl over hot water, spread evenly over top of each cake.

2 Whip cream until firm peaks form. Fold 1 cup of the whipped cream into remaining chestnut spread. Place 1 cake onto board, chocolate side up, spread evenly with chestnut mixture, top with other cake, chocolate side down. Spread remaining cream over cake. Decorate with strawberries and toffee strands just before serving.

BRANDIED CHESTNUT CAKE

This cake is at its best made and eaten on the same day. The toffee strands will dissolve if refrigerated. Unfilled cake will freeze for up to a month. This recipe is not suitable to microwave.

3 Toffee: Combine sugar and water in saucepan, stir constantly over heat without boiling until sugar is dissolved. Bring to the boil, boil rapidly without stirring for about 10 minutes or until toffee is golden brown. Using a metal spoon, drizzle toffee in thin stream, backward and forward, over lightly oiled trays. When set, break off small pieces and place on cake.

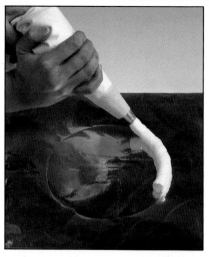

2 Pipe a circle of meringue on each of the 3 remaining oven trays, these form the wall of the vacherin. Bake all 4 trays of meringues in a very slow oven. The thick base will take about 2 hours, the 3 rings about 1 hour. Meringue must be crisp and dry to touch. Cool in oven with door ajar.

VACHERIN

A Vacherin is a basket made from meringue and filled with cream and fruit. You will need 2 ovens for this recipe, or a fan forced oven which will accommodate 4 trays at a time. Some ovens are wide enough to take 2 trays, which hold 2 lots of meringue on 1 tray. Vacherin can be made several days beforehand; store in an airtight container. Fill with cream up to 4 hours before serving. This recipe is not suitable to freeze or microwave.

3 egg whites
¾ cup castor sugar
½ teaspoon white vinegar
4 egg whites, extra
1¼ cups castor sugar, extra
1 teaspoon white vinegar, extra
COINTREAU CREAM
2 x 300ml cartons thickened cream
⅓ cup sour cream
¼ cup castor sugar
2 tablespoons Cointreau
250g punnet strawberries, halved

1 Cover 4 oven trays with foil, mark an 18cm circle on each; a plate is ideal to use as a guide.

Beat egg whites in small bowl with electric mixer until soft peaks form, gradually add sugar and vinegar, beat until sugar is dissolved. Fill piping bag fitted with 1cm tube with meringue. Starting from just inside the marked circle on one tray, pipe a concentric circle of meringue to form a base of meringue, smooth top with spatula.

3 Beat extra egg whites in small bowl with electric mixer until soft peaks form, gradually add extra sugar and extra vinegar, beat until sugar is dissolved, about 10 minutes. Fill piping bag fitted with a fluted tube with meringue. Place meringue base onto foil covered tray, use a little meringue to secure each ring in position as shown. Fill any gaps with meringue. Working from the base to the top, pipe vertical lines of meringue up the side and slightly over the top of the vacherin. Bake in very slow oven for about 1½ hours or until crisp and dry. Turn oven off, cool in oven with door ajar.

Cointreau Cream: Combine all ingredients except strawberries in medium bowl, beat with electric mixer until soft peaks form. Just before required, stir in strawberries. Fill vacherin with Cointreau cream. Decorate with extra whipped cream and fruit if desired.

Serves 8.

See Ratatouille Omelette (page 22) for information on seasoning an omelette pan. A Soufflé Omelette is not difficult to make, but make sure you have everything ready, the hot griller, the hot pan and the lucky recipient. Do not have an exhaust fan operating when flaming the rum. This recipe is not suitable to freeze or microwave.

30g butter
2 tablespoons brown sugar
¼ cup fruit mince
1 tablespoon rum
1 teaspoon grated lemon rind
OMELETTE
2 eggs, separated
2 teaspoons water
1 tablespoon castor sugar
15g butter

1 Melt butter in small frying pan, add sugar, cook, stirring, without boiling, until sugar is dissolved, stir in fruit mince, add rum, ignite rum; when the flame subsides, stir in lemon rind. Keep the topping warm while preparing the omelette.

2 **Omelette:** Whisk egg yolks, water and sugar together in large bowl. Beat egg whites in small bowl until soft peaks form, fold egg whites gently into egg yolk mixture in 2 lots.

3 Preheat grill to high. Heat omelette pan, add butter to pan, swirl butter

SOUFFLE OMELETTE

evenly around pan. Pour in egg mixture, cook over high heat for about 20 seconds or until base of omelette begins to brown. Place pan under hot griller, grill omelette for about a further 20 seconds or until the top is set. Working quickly, use a spatula or egg slide, slide the omelette onto serving plate, folding the omelette in half at the same time. Top with fruit mince mixture, serve immediately.
Serves 1.

PEACH CLAFOUTI

This simple dessert consists of a pancake batter poured over fruit and baked. Any type of canned or stewed fruit can be used. This recipe is unsuitable to freeze or microwave.

825g can peach slices, drained
⅓ cup plain flour
2 tablespoons self-raising flour
¼ cup castor sugar
3 eggs, lightly beaten
2 cups milk
1 teaspoon vanilla essence

2 Combine sifted flours and sugar in bowl, gradually stir in eggs, then milk and essence, mix to a smooth batter or blend or process mixture.

3 Pour batter into dish over the back of a spoon. Bake in moderate oven for about 50 minutes or until a knife inserted in centre comes out clean. Serve warm with cream or icecream.
Serves 6.

1 Grease a shallow ovenproof dish, place peaches in dish.

Chair: Australian East India Company; cushion and linen: Les Olivades; dish: The Bay Tree

COEUR A LA CREME

Coeur a la Crème is usually set in heart-shaped moulds, available from specialty cookware shops. These moulds have small holes in the base to allow excess moisture to escape while dessert is setting. Individual mousse dishes may be used instead. Moulds are lined with muslin for easy removal; cut muslin slightly larger then moulds. Coeur à la Crème can be made a day ahead of serving; keep covered and refrigerated. This recipe is unsuitable to freeze.

250g packet cream cheese
2 tablespoons castor sugar
1 teaspoon vanilla essence
2 teaspoons grated lemon rind
⅔ cup sour cream
⅔ cup thickened cream
PASSIONFRUIT COULIS
4 passionfruit
1 tablespoon lemon juice
1 tablespoon icing sugar,
  approximately

1 Beat softened cream cheese, sugar, essence and rind in small bowl with electric mixer until smooth.

2 Lightly fold in sour cream and whipped cream.

3 Fill muslin-lined moulds with cheese mixture, fold over excess muslin to cover top of cheese mixture, refrigerate overnight.

Unmould crèmes onto serving plates, remove muslin. Serve with passionfruit coulis, extra whipped cream and fresh fruit if desired.

Passionfruit Coulis: Combine passionfruit pulp, lemon juice and sifted icing sugar to taste; mix well.

ALMOND BLANCMANGE

We ground our own blanched almonds for this recipe. Blancmange can be made a day ahead of serving. Sauce must be made just before serving. This recipe is unsuitable to freeze.

1 cup ground almonds
¾ cup water
½ cup milk
½ cup sugar
2 teaspoons gelatine
300ml carton thickened cream
GRAND MARNIER SAUCE
1 egg
2 egg yolks
⅓ cup sugar
2 tablespoons Grand Marnier
½ cup thickened cream

1 Combine almonds, ½ cup of the water, milk and sugar in small saucepan, stir constantly over heat without boiling until sugar is dissolved. Bring to the boil, reduce heat, simmer 3 minutes (or microwave on HIGH 2 minutes). Strain almond mixture through a sieve lined with cheese cloth over a bowl, squeeze liquid from almond mixture, discard almond pulp.

Sprinkle gelatine over remaining water, dissolve over hot water (or microwave on HIGH about 30 seconds), stir into almond liquid; cool to room temperature.

2 Fold whipped cream lightly into almond liquid, spoon into lightly oiled moulds (½ cup capacity), cover, refrigerate several hours or overnight. Unmould onto serving plates, serve with sauce, decorate with finely shredded orange rind if desired.
Grand Marnier Sauce: Combine egg, egg yolks, sugar and Grand Marnier in top of double saucepan or bowl, whisk over simmering water until thick and frothy; cool to room temperature. Fold in lightly whipped cream.

Serves 6.

Table: Barbara's House & Garden; china: Southdown from Royal Doulton; linen: Jeffcoat Stevenson

Prepare this dessert at least a day ahead; it will keep, covered, in freezer for up to a month.

6 eggs
1¼ cups castor sugar
300ml carton thickened cream
¾ cup dried apricots
¾ cup water
60g dark chocolate, grated
2 tablespoons Cointreau

1 Whisk eggs and sugar in a heat-proof bowl or in the top of a double saucepan over simmering water for about 10 minutes or until foamy, cool to room temperature. Beat cream in small bowl until soft peaks form, fold into egg mixture. Pour into a lamington pan, cover, freeze several hours or until firm.

CHOC-APRICOT ICECREAM BOMBE

2 Combine apricots and water in a saucepan, bring to the boil, reduce heat, cover, simmer 10 minutes or until apricots are tender. Blend or process until smooth, transfer to large bowl, cool. Beat half the frozen icecream in small bowl with electric mixer until smooth, stir into apricot mixture.

3 Line base and side of a 6 cup pudding basin with strips of foil, pour in two-thirds of the apricot icecream; return both portions to freezer. When icecream in basin is firm, spread evenly and smoothly up side of basin, freeze until firm.

4 Beat remaining half of plain ice-cream in small bowl with electric mixer until smooth. Stir in chocolate and Cointreau, pour into basin; freeze until firm. Soften remaining apricot ice-cream, spread over chocolate ice-cream, freeze overnight.

2 Beat butter and essence together in small bowl with electric mixer until smooth and creamy, gradually add sifted icing sugar, beat until mixture is light and fluffy, beat in chestnut.

3 Layer sponge with chestnut mixture, finishing with a sponge layer.

4 **Chocolate Topping:** Melt chocolate and butter over hot water, cool to room temperature, stand until thickened. Spread chocolate mixture over cake, refrigerate until set. Decorate with grated white chocolate.

CHESTNUT RUM CAKE

This recipe required a Génoise Sponge (see page 108 for recipe). This cake can be made a day in advance; cover, refrigerate until required. This recipe is not suitable to freeze or microwave.

20cm Génoise Sponge
2 tablespoons rum
60g butter
1 teaspoon vanilla essence
¾ cup icing sugar
½ cup chestnut spread
CHOCOLATE TOPPING
150g dark chocolate, chopped
125g unsalted butter

1 Split sponge into 3 layers. Brush each layer with rum.

Fabric: Les Olivades; plate: Studio Haus

Fabric: Les Olivades; china: Petit Fleur from Villeroy & Boch

60g butter
1 tablespoon grated lime rind
⅓ cup castor sugar
1 tablespoon cornflour
2 tablespoons plain flour
1 tablespoon lime juice
1 cup milk
4 eggs, separated
2 egg whites
2 tablespoons castor sugar, extra
STRAWBERRY CREAM
1 cup strawberries
½ cup sour cream
2 tablespoons icing sugar

LIME SOUFFLE

Soufflé can be made several hours in advance up to the end of step 2 and egg whites folded through just before baking. Strawberry Cream can be made several hours in advance; keep covered in refrigerator. Soufflés can also be cooked in 6 individual dishes (1 cup capacity). Bake in moderately hot oven for about 15 minutes. This recipe is unsuitable to freeze or microwave.

1 Cream butter, rind and sugar in small bowl with electric mixer until light and fluffy, beat in sifted flours and lime juice. Heat milk in small saucepan, stir in spoonfuls of the creamed butter mixture; stir constantly over heat until mixture boils and thickens.

2 Mix in egg yolks, transfer mixture to large bowl.

3 Beat the 6 egg whites in large bowl until soft peaks form. Fold egg whites into custard mixture in 2 lots. Grease a 20cm soufflé dish, sprinkle base and side with extra sugar, carefully pour soufflé mixture into dish. Bake in moderately hot oven for about 35 minutes. Serve immediately with strawberry cream.
Strawberry Cream: Blend or process all ingredients until smooth.
Serves 6.

GATEAU ST HONORE

We have made individual gâteaux, they are a little time consuming, but well worth the effort. Assemble the gâteaux as close to serving time as possible, up to 2 hours is ideal. Make the toffee only when you are ready to assemble the gâteaux, it will set quickly and will not re-melt without burning. The pastry bases (with rings) and puffs can be cooked up to a week ahead and stored in an airtight container. If the puffs soften a little, it means you should have dried them out more, but they can be re-crisped in a moderate oven for a few minutes. Crème Pâtissière can be made up to 2 days before required, but best results will be obtained from folding in the egg white mixture just before the gâteaux are filled. This recipe is unsuitable to freeze or microwave.

CREME PATISSIERE
4 egg yolks
2 tablespoons castor sugar
2 tablespoons plain flour
2 tablespoons cornflour
1¾ cups milk
2 tablespoons Grand Marnier
2 egg whites
2 tablespoons castor sugar, extra
300ml carton thickened cream
PATE SUCRE
1½ cups plain flour
1 tablespoon icing sugar
90g butter
1 egg yolk
1 tablespoon water, approximately
CHOUX PASTRY
1 cup water
75g butter, chopped
1 cup plain flour
4 eggs
TOFFEE
1½ cups sugar
¾ cup water

1 Roll pâté sucre out thinly on lightly floured surface (or between pieces of greaseproof paper or plastic wrap). Cut out 6 x 9cm rounds, place rounds on lightly greased oven trays, refrigerate 20 minutes. Place choux pastry into piping bag fitted with a small plain tube, pipe rings onto pastry bases, just inside the edges. Prick pâté sucre bases in the centres with fork.

2 Pipe remaining choux pastry into small rounds (about the size of a hazelnut) onto lightly greased oven trays. Smooth top of puffs with wet finger. Bake in moderately hot oven for about 15 minutes. Bake bases in moderately hot oven for about 25 minutes, or until lightly browned. Make a slit in each side of the choux pastry rings — this is to allow steam to escape. Return bases to oven for about another 5 minutes, or until rings feel crisp and dry. Remove from trays to wire rack to cool. Carefully dip bases of small puffs into toffee, position on pastry rings, hold in position for a few seconds until set. Spoon a little more toffee carefully over the top of the puffs.

3 Use a small pointed knife to make a small hole at the base of each puff,

inside each ring. Place crème pâtissière into a piping bag fitted with a small plain tube, pipe crème pâtissière into each puff.

4 Dip a teaspoon into remaining toffee, quickly touch the tops of the toffee-coated puffs and pull threads of toffee in several directions. Fill gâteaux with crème pâtissière, then top with whipped cream.

Crème Pâtissière: Combine egg yolks, sugar, flour, cornflour and ¼ cup of the milk in small bowl of electric mixer, beat until combined. Bring remaining milk to boil in a saucepan, gradually add to egg yolk mixture while mixer is operating. Return mixture to saucepan, stir constantly over heat until mixture boils and thickens, transfer to large bowl. Stir in Grand Marnier, cover, cool to room temperature. Beat egg whites until soft peaks form, gradually add extra sugar, beat until dissolved. Lightly fold egg white mixture into custard mixture.

Pâté Sucre: Sift flour and icing sugar into large bowl, rub in butter. Add egg yolk and enough water to make ingredients cling together. Knead quickly and lightly until smooth, cover, refrigerate 30 minutes.

Choux Pastry: Combine butter and water in saucepan, bring to the boil, boil until butter is melted. Add flour all at once, beat vigorously over heat with wooden spoon until mixture leaves the side of the pan. Transfer mixture to small bowl of electric mixer, beat in eggs one at a time, beating well after each addition; mixture should be smooth and glossy.

Toffee: Combine sugar and water in saucepan, stir constantly over heat without boiling until sugar is dissolved. Bring to the boil, boil rapidly uncovered, without stirring, for about 10 minutes or until mixture turns a light golden brown. Stand saucepan of toffee in another pan of hot water to keep it as runny as possible during the assembling of the gâteaux.
Makes 6.

Linen: Balmain Linen and Lace; china: Golden Cove from Noritake; cutlery: Mikasa; tray: Kerry Trollope Antiques.

CREME BRULEE

This recipe can be made up to the end of step 1 a day ahead of serving; it is not suitable to freeze or microwave.

2 x 300ml cartons thickened cream
6 egg yolks
¼ cup castor sugar
2 teaspoons vanilla essence
¼ cup crystal sugar

1 Pour cream into a saucepan, bring to the boil. Combine egg yolks, castor sugar and essence in top half of double saucepan or heatproof bowl, beat with electric mixer or rotary beater until pale and thick. Gradually pour in hot cream while motor is operating. Place mixture over simmering water, stir constantly until mixture thickly coats the wooden spoon. Spoon into 4 ovenproof dishes (¾ cup capacity); refrigerate until set.

2 Sprinkle crystal sugar over set custards about 1 hour before serving. Place dishes into a lamington pan.

3 Pack ice cubes around dishes, place under preheated grill, grill until sugar is lightly browned. Refrigerate until ready to serve.
  Serves 4.

Table: Freedom Furniture; spoon: George Jensen

FRENCH FRUIT FLAN

Pastry case can be made the day before required, store in an airtight container. Baked unfilled pastry case can be frozen for up to 2 months. Fruit Flan is at its best eaten on the day it is made. This recipe is unsuitable to microwave.

Grey china: Taitu from Lifestyle Imports; white plate: by Pillivuyt from Hale Imports

PASTRY
1 cup plain flour
1 tablespoon icing sugar
90g butter
1 egg yolk
1 tablespoon lemon juice,
  approximately
CREME PATISSIERE
1¼ cups milk
1 egg
2 egg yolks
1 tablespoon plain flour
1 tablespoon cornflour
¼ cup castor sugar
1 teaspoon vanilla essence
TOPPING
425g can apricot halves
425g can black cherries, drained
250g punnet strawberries
1 kiwi fruit, sliced
1 tablespoon brandy
1 tablespoon arrowroot

1 Pastry: Sift flour and sugar into large bowl, rub in butter. Add egg yolk and enough lemon juice to mix to a firm dough. Press ingredients together into a smooth ball, cover, refrigerate 30 minutes. Roll pastry on lightly floured surface or between pieces of plastic wrap or greaseproof paper large enough to line 23cm flan tin. Ease pastry gently into side of tin with fingers. Roll rolling pin over top of tin to cut off excess pastry, refrigerate 20 minutes. Cover pastry case with greaseproof paper, fill with dried beans or rice. Bake in moderately hot oven for 7 minutes, remove paper and rice, bake further 7 minutes or until lightly browned, cool to room temperature.

2 Crème Pâtissière: Combine ¼ cup of the milk, egg, egg yolks, flour, cornflour and sugar in processor, process until combined. Place remaining milk in saucepan, bring to the boil. Pour hot milk gradually into processor while motor is operating, process until smooth. Return mixture to saucepan, stir constantly over heat until mixture boils and thickens. Remove from heat, stir in essence, cool to room temperature. Spread crème pâtissière into pastry case. Drain apricots, slice thinly, reserve syrup. Arrange fruit decoratively over crème. Blend arrowroot with about 2 tablespoons of the reserved syrup in saucepan, stir in brandy and remaining syrup. Stir constantly over heat until mixture boils and thickens. Brush glaze over fruit, refrigerate flan several hours before serving.

2 Whisk egg yolks, sugar and Tia Maria in a bowl, whisk in coffee-flavoured cream. Pour mixture into individual ovenproof dishes (⅓ cup capacity). Place dishes into a lamington pan. Pour enough hot water into the pan to come halfway up the side of the dishes. Cover with foils or lids, bake in slow oven for about 20 minutes or until mixture is just set; cool, refrigerate before serving.

COFFEE POTS DE CREME

Pots de Crème can be made the day before serving; cover, refrigerate. Praline can be made ahead and stored in an airtight container; it keeps indefinitely. Tia Maria and Kahlua are coffee-flavoured liqueurs. This recipe is unsuitable to freeze or microwave.

2 x 300ml cartons thickened cream
½ cup roasted coffee beans
6 egg yolks
¼ cup castor sugar
2 teaspoons Tia Maria or Kahlua
PRALINE
2 tablespoons slivered almonds
¼ cup sugar
1 tablespoon water

1 Pour cream into saucepan, bring to the boil, add coffee beans, reduce heat, simmer gently 3 minutes, remove from heat, stand 30 minutes; strain.

3 **Praline:** Place almonds into a saucepan, stir constantly over heat until lightly browned, spread evenly onto a lightly greased oven tray. Combine sugar and water in same pan, stir constantly over heat without boiling until sugar is dissolved. Boil rapidly without stirring until mixture turns golden brown. Remove from heat, allow bubbles to subside, pour over almonds, chop roughly when set. Decorate pots de crème with extra whipped cream and praline.
Serves 8.

COUNTRY APPLE PIE

Baked unfilled pastry case can be frozen for up to 2 months. We used Granny Smith apples in this recipe. Apple Filling can be prepared the day before required. This recipe is not suitable to microwave.

PASTRY
- 1¾ cups plain flour
- ¼ cup self-raising flour
- 1 tablespoon icing sugar
- 125g butter, chopped
- 1 egg, lightly beaten
- 2 tablespoons lemon juice, approximately
- 1 egg white
- 2 tablespoons apricot jam

FILLING
- 5 large apples, thinly sliced
- ¼ cup water
- 2 tablespoons sugar
- 1 teaspoon grated lemon rind

1 Pastry: Sift flours and sugar into bowl, rub in butter. Add the egg and enough lemon juice to mix to a firm dough, cover, refrigerate pastry for 30 minutes.

2 Roll three-quarters of the pastry between sheets of plastic wrap, greaseproof or baking paper until large enough to line a deep 23cm flan tin. Trim edges with rolling pin, refrigerate pastry case 30 minutes. Refrigerate remaining pastry and any scraps of pastry while preparing filling. Cover pastry case with greaseproof paper, fill with dried beans or rice. Bake in moderately hot oven 7 minutes, remove paper and beans, bake for a further 7 minutes. Spread cold filling into pastry case.

3 Roll remaining pastry out to 3mm thickness, cut into 1cm strips. Brush edge of pastry with egg white. Place pastry strips over filling in a lattice pattern, press gently against edge of pastry, brush with egg white. Bake pie in moderately hot oven for about 20 minutes or until pastry is golden brown. Brush the pie with warmed sieved jam.

Filling: Combine apples and water in large saucepan, bring to the boil, reduce heat, simmer covered over low heat for about 5 minutes or until apples are tender. Stir in sugar and rind; cool to room temperature, drain.

RICH CHOCOLATE MOUSSE

Mousse can be made several days ahead of serving; keep covered in refrigerator. Serve with whipped cream and chocolate curls. This recipe is not suitable to freeze.

300g dark chocolate, chopped
300ml carton thickened cream
2 tablespoons rum
4 egg whites
⅓ cup castor sugar
½ cup thickened cream, extra

2 Beat egg whites in small bowl with electric mixer until soft peaks form, gradually add sugar a tablespoon at a time, beating well after each addition.

3 Fold egg white mixture through chocolate mixture in 2 lots.

1 Process chocolate until finely grated. Heat cream to just below boiling point, gradually add cream to chocolate while motor is operating; add rum, process until smooth. Transfer chocolate mixture to large bowl.

4 Whip extra cream until soft peaks form, fold cream through chocolate mixture. Pour mousse into serving glasses. Refrigerate mousse several hours or overnight.
Serves 8.

Glasses: The Bay Tree; linen: Jeffcoat Stevenson; basket: Keyhole Furniture

CHOUX PASTRY
75g butter, chopped
1 cup water
1 cup plain flour
4 eggs
TOPPING
⅔ cup flaked almonds
250g dark chocolate, chopped
30g butter
2 tablespoons hot water
CREME PATISSIERE
1 egg, separated
1 egg yolk
¼ cup castor sugar
1 cup milk
1 tablespoon plain flour
1 tablespoon cornflour
1 tablespoon castor sugar, extra
1 tablespoon rum
300ml carton thickened cream

1 Combine butter and water in saucepan, bring to the boil; boil until butter is melted. Add sifted flour all at once, stir vigorously over heat until mixture leaves side of saucepan. Transfer mixture to small bowl of electric mixer, add eggs one at a time beating well after each addition; beat until smooth and glossy. Lightly grease an oven tray, mark a 20cm circle on tray. Fill piping bag (without a tube) with mixture, pipe thickly around edge of circle. Bake in hot oven 10 minutes, reduce heat to moderate, bake further 20 minutes or until golden brown and crisp. Cut pastry ring in half, return to oven for a few minutes to dry out completely; cool on wire rack.

PARIS-BREST

The baked pastry ring can be made up to a week in advance and stored in an airtight container. It can be frozen for a month and recrisped in a moderate oven for about 5 minutes, cooled and filled as close to serving time as possible. This recipe is not suitable to microwave.

2 Place bottom half of pastry onto plate, fill with crème pâtissière. Top with whipped cream.

3 Topping: Toast almonds on oven tray in moderate oven for about 5 minutes. Melt chocolate and butter over hot water, stir in hot water, spread chocolate over top half of pastry; sprinkle with almonds, refrigerate until firm. Place top on base, dust with sifted icing sugar just before serving.

Crème Pâtissière: Combine egg yolks, sugar, ¼ cup of the milk and flours in a small bowl, beat until smooth. Bring remaining milk to boil, gradually stir into egg mixture, beat until smooth. Return the mixture to saucepan, stir constantly over heat until mixture boils and thickens, remove from heat; cover, cool to room temperature. Beat egg white until soft peaks form, gradually add extra sugar, beat until dissolved. Lightly fold the egg white mixture and rum into crème; then gently fold in the whipped cream.

1 Toast almonds on oven tray in moderate oven for about 5 minutes; cool. Beat egg whites in small bowl with electric mixer until soft peaks form. Gradually add sugar, beat until dissolved between each addition.

Fold in sifted flour, then almonds. Spread evenly and smoothly onto 2 greased and lined 23cm springform pan bases. Bake in slow oven 20 minutes or until firm to touch. Stand 5 minutes before removing from bases.

2 **Coffee Cream:** Combine custard powder and sugar in a saucepan. Gradually stir in milk, stir constantly over heat until mixture boils and thickens. Cover top of custard with plastic wrap to prevent skin forming, cool to room temperature. Dissolve coffee in water, cool. Beat butter and extra sugar in small bowl with electric mixer until light and creamy, gradually add cooled custard and coffee mixture; beat until smooth between additions.

3 Spread a meringue layer with half the coffee cream, top with remaining meringue layer. Spread top and side with remaining coffee cream. Refrigerate until firm. Decorate with whipped cream, strawberries and grated chocolate if desired.

COFFEE DACQUOISE

Dacquoise will cut more easily if made the day before required. This recipe is not suitable to freeze or microwave.

1 cup packaged ground almonds
2 egg whites
½ cup castor sugar
2 tablespoons plain flour
COFFEE CREAM
¼ cup custard powder
¼ cup sugar
1 cup milk
1 tablespoon instant coffee powder
2 tablespoons hot water
250g unsalted butter
¼ cup sugar, extra

Dresser: Kerry Trollope; china: Arco Weiss by Villeroy & Boch; linen: Balmain Linen and Lace

Flan can be made the day before required, keep covered in refrigerator. We used Granny Smith apples in this recipe. This recipe is not suitable to freeze or microwave.

FRENCH APPLE FLAN

BISCUIT PASTRY
90g butter
¼ cup castor sugar
1 egg
1¼ cups plain flour
¼ cup self-raising flour
FILLING
375ml jar apple sauce
2 large apples
1 teaspoon grated lemon rind
2 tablespoons lemon juice
2 tablespoons apricot jam
1 tablespoon brandy

smooth, add sugar and egg, beat only until combined. Stir in half the sifted flours then stir in remaining flours until ingredients just cling together. Knead gently on lightly floured surface until smooth. Over handling of this pastry will cause it to toughen and crack when rolled out. Wrap pastry in plastic wrap, refrigerate 30 minutes.

proof paper, fill with dried beans or rice. Bake in moderately hot oven for 7 minutes, remove paper and beans, bake further 10 minutes or until lightly browned; cool.

3 Spread apple sauce into pastry case. Peel and core apples, cut into wedges. Slice wedges thinly, toss apple slices in combined lemon rind and juice. Overlap apple slices evenly over apple sauce. Bake in moderate oven for about 30 minutes or until apples are tender. Combine jam and brandy in small saucepan, stir over low heat until warm; strain. Brush over apples; serve warm or cold.

2 Roll pastry on lightly floured surface (or between pieces of plastic wrap, greaseproof or baking paper) large enough to line a 23cm flan tin; trim edge with rolling pin. Refrigerate 30 minutes. Cover pastry with grease-

1 **Biscuit Pastry:** Cream butter in small bowl with electric mixer until

CHOCOLATE CREAM CAKE

We decorated this cake with chocolate strawberry leaves (see Génoise Sponge page 108 for how to coat rose leaves), strawberries and chocolate curls. Kirsch is a cherry-flavoured liqueur, although you can use your favourite liqueur. The undecorated, unfilled cake can be frozen for up to 2 months. The butter cream can be made a week ahead; allow it to return to room temperature before beating, to return it to its original consistency. Cake can be completed a day before required; keep refrigerated. This recipe is unsuitable to microwave.

1 tablespoon instant coffee powder
⅓ cup cocoa
⅔ cup hot water
125g butter
1 cup castor sugar
3 eggs, separated
1 teaspoon bicarbonate of soda
⅓ cup sour cream
1½ cups plain flour
⅓ cup castor sugar, extra
CHOCOLATE BUTTER CREAM
250g dark chocolate, chopped
185g unsalted butter, chopped
KIRSCH CREAM
300ml carton thickened cream
250g punnet strawberries, chopped
1 tablespoon Kirsch

1 Grease a deep 23cm cake pan, line base with paper; grease paper. Blend coffee and sifted cocoa with water in bowl until smooth. Combine soft butter, sugar, egg yolks and half the cocoa mixture in small bowl, beat with electric mixer until light in colour and creamy. Transfer mixture to large bowl, stir in combined sifted soda and sour cream, remaining cocoa mixture, then sifted flour. Beat egg whites until soft peaks form, gradually add extra sugar, beat until dissolved, lightly fold into cake mixture in 2 lots. Spread mixture into prepared pan, bake in moderate oven for about 1 hour. Turn onto wire rack to cool. Split cake into 3 layers, join layers on serving plate with Kirsch cream, cover, refrigerate overnight or while preparing butter cream.

2 **Chocolate Butter Cream:** Combine chocolate and butter in top of double saucepan or bowl, melt over hot water, stir until smooth. Transfer mixture to large bowl, cool. Stir occasionally during cooling. The time this cream takes to thicken to a spreading and piping consistency depends on the room temperature. It can be refrigerated to cool more quickly, stir every 5 minutes to prevent mixture setting around the edge of the bowl. Spread top and side of cake with chocolate cream, pipe rosettes on top if desired.

3 To make chocolate curls, spread 125g of melted dark chocolate onto a marble or laminated surface, cool chocolate to room temperature. Push the blade of a sharp heavy knife at about a 45 degree angle, across the surface of the chocolate. All curls will be different shapes and lengths. Mistakes can be remelted and used again in the same way or for any other recipe using melted chocolate.
Kirsch Cream: Beat cream until thick, fold in strawberries and Kirsch.

ORANGE CREME CAKE

You will need a Génoise Sponge for this recipe (see page 108). This recipe is not suitable to freeze or microwave.

3 cups sugar
4 cups water
4 oranges, sliced
20cm round Génoise Sponge
CREME PATISSIERE
6 egg yolks
⅔ cup castor sugar
2 cups milk
2 tablespoons plain flour
2 tablespoons cornflour
1 teaspoon vanilla essence
CREME CHANTILLY
300ml carton thickened cream
1 tablespoon icing sugar
1 teaspoon vanilla essence
ORANGE SYRUP
½ cup water
⅓ cup sugar
2 tablespoons orange juice
1 tablespoon Grand Marnier

1 Combine sugar and water in large saucepan, stir over heat without boiling until sugar is dissolved. Add oranges, bring to the boil, reduce heat, simmer gently uncovered for about 2 hours. Drain oranges, cool, drain on absorbent paper.

Grease a deep 23cm round cake pan, sprinkle with a little extra castor sugar. Cover base and half-way up side of pan with half the orange slices.

2 Chop remaining orange slices, add to crème pâtissière; mix well; fold crème chantilly into crème pâtissière; spread half the crème mixture over oranges in pan.

3 Split sponge in half. Place 1 layer in pan on crème mixture, brush with half the warm orange syrup. Spread remaining crème mixture over sponge, top with remaining sponge and syrup.

4 Cover sponge with a dinner plate, weigh the sponge down with a few cans. Refrigerate cake several hours or overnight. To serve cake, quickly dip pan into hot water; invert carefully onto serving plate.

Crème Pâtissière: Combine egg yolks, sugar, ½ cup of the milk, flour and cornflour in large bowl of electric mixer; beat until smooth. Bring remaining milk to boil in saucepan; gradually add to egg yolk mixture while motor is operating. Return mixture to saucepan, stir constantly over heat until mixture boils and thickens. Remove from heat, add essence; beat mixture until smooth; cover surface with plastic wrap, cool to room temperature.

Crème Chantilly: Beat cream, sifted icing sugar and essence until firm peaks form.

Orange Syrup: Combine water and sugar in a saucepan, stir constantly over heat without boiling until sugar is dissolved. Bring to the boil, reduce heat, simmer, uncovered 3 minutes. Stir in orange juice and Grand Marnier. Use while warm.

PROFITEROLES

China: Grenville by Royal Crown Derby from Royal Doulton; linen: Hampshire and Loundes

Profiteroles are made from choux pastry; they are also known as puffs. The cooked dried out puffs will keep in an airtight container for about a week or may be frozen for about a month. Re-crisp puffs in a moderate oven for a few minutes. Cool, fill as close to serving time as possible. Chocolate Sauce can be made a day ahead. This recipe is not suitable to microwave.

75g butter, chopped
1 cup water
1 cup plain flour
4 eggs
300ml carton thickened cream
CHOCOLATE SAUCE
1 egg
2 egg yolks
⅓ cup sugar
1 teaspoon grated orange rind
2 tablespoons Grand Marnier
60g dark chocolate
½ cup thickened cream

1 Combine butter and water in saucepan, bring to the boil. When butter is melted and water boiling rapidly, add sifted flour all at once; stir vigorously until mixture leaves side of saucepan and forms a smooth ball.

2 Transfer mixture to small bowl of electric mixer, add eggs one at a time, beating well after each addition. Mixture should be glossy.

3 Drop teaspoonfuls of mixture about 5cm apart onto greased oven trays. Bake in hot oven 10 minutes, reduce heat to moderate, bake further 15 minutes or until puffs are lightly browned and crisp. Make a small slit in the side of puffs to allow steam to escape, return to moderate oven for about 10 minutes or until dry. Cool to room temperature, cut in half; remove any soft mixture from centre. Fill puffs with whipped cream and serve with chocolate sauce.

Chocolate Sauce: Combine egg, yolks, sugar, rind and Grand Marnier in top of double saucepan or bowl over simmering water, whisk for about 10 minutes or until thick and frothy; cool to room temperature. Melt chocolate over hot water; stir into egg mixture, cool to room temperature. Beat cream until soft peaks form, gently fold into chocolate mixture.

Makes about 30.

MOCHA LOG CAKE

This dessert is best made the day before required, to allow the layers to soften slightly; it is not suitable to freeze or microwave.

310g unsalted butter
¾ cup castor sugar
2½ cups plain flour
¾ cup cocoa
300ml carton thickened cream
CHOCOLATE FILLING
60g unsalted butter
½ cup castor sugar
¼ cup plain flour
2 cups milk
1 tablespoon instant coffee powder
¼ cup hot water
100g dark chocolate, grated

1 Lightly grease 2 oven trays. Cream butter and sugar in large bowl with electric mixer until light and fluffy. Stir in sifted flour and cocoa. Knead dough gently, press into a smooth ball. Divide dough into 4 pieces, wrap each in plastic wrap, refrigerate 30 minutes. Roll each piece of dough between 2 sheets of plastic wrap to a 10cm x 20cm rectangle. Place dough onto prepared trays. Bake in moderate oven for about 12 minutes.

2 While layers are still warm, lift from trays to board and trim edges to make the layers all the same size. Return layers to trays to cool.

3 Chocolate Filling: Melt butter in small saucepan, stir in sugar and sifted flour, stir over heat 1 minute. Gradually stir in milk and blended coffee and water, stir constantly over heat until mixture boils and thickens. Reduce heat, simmer, stirring for 1 minute. Remove from heat, stir in chocolate; cover, cool to room temperature.

4 Place a chocolate layer on board, spread evenly with one-third of the filling. Repeat layering, finishing with fourth chocolate layer. Cover, refrigerate overnight. Next day, cover completely with whipped cream, decorate with chocolate curls if desired.

Etched glass: Architectural Heritage; linen: Jeffcoat Stevenson; china: Forget me not by Royal Worcester; platter: Copenhagen from Orrefors

Table: Wentworth Antiques; china: Heather by Royal Doulton; glass platter: Mayfair by Mikasa

ALMOND JALOUSIE

375g packet puff pastry
1 tablespoon apricot jam
1 egg white
1 tablespoon sugar
ALMOND FILLING
30g butter
1 cup flaked almonds
2 tablespoons castor sugar
1 teaspoon vanilla essence
2 egg yolks
2 teaspoons plain flour

Jalousie is best made on the day of serving. Serve with whipped cream if desired. This recipe is not suitable to freeze or microwave.

25cm rectangle. Place on an oven tray, spread centre with warmed sieved jam. Place almond filling on pastry leaving about a 2cm border around the edge.

1 Cut pastry in half, roll 1 half to a rectangle, trim neatly to a 12cm x

2 Roll remaining pastry to rectangle, trim edges neatly to a 13cm x 27cm rectangle, fold in half lengthways. Brush pastry on both sides lightly with egg white, this will help prevent pastry from splitting during cooking. Cut through folded edge of pastry at 2cm intervals leaving a 2cm border down long side of pastry strip.

3 Glaze around edge of pastry strip on oven tray with egg white. Carefully unfold cut pastry strip, place over almond filling. Press edges of pastry together using thumb and back of knife to make decorative edge. Brush evenly with egg white, sprinkle with sugar. Bake in hot oven 5 minutes, reduce to moderately hot, bake 10 minutes or until golden brown.

Almond Filling: Melt butter in saucepan, add almonds, stir constantly over heat until almonds are lightly browned. Process almond mixture with remaining ingredients until smooth.

ALMOND CHOCOLATE CAKE

It is correct that this cake is made without using flour; it can be kept refrigerated for up to 3 days. The un-iced cake can be frozen for up to 2 months. This recipe is unsuitable to microwave.

125g butter
¾ cup castor sugar
6 eggs, separated
125g dark chocolate, grated
2 cups (250g) packaged ground almonds
⅓ cup stale white breadcrumbs
1 tablespoon dark rum
90g dark chocolate, extra
30g butter, extra

1 Grease a deep 23cm round cake pan, line base with paper; grease paper. Cream butter and sugar in small bowl with electric mixer until light and fluffy, add egg yolks, beat well.

2 Transfer mixture to large bowl, stir in chocolate, almonds, breadcrumbs and rum.

3 Beat egg whites until soft peaks form, fold through almond mixture in 2 lots. Pour into prepared pan, bake in moderate oven about 50 minutes. Stand 5 minutes before turning onto wire rack to cool. Melt extra chocolate and extra butter over hot water, cool before spreading over cake.

China: Saturn by Sasaki from Dansab; mat, cushion, table: Australian East India Company

AMBASSADOR CAKE

This recipe requires a Génoise Sponge (see page 108). It can be made up to 2 days ahead. This recipe is not suitable to freeze or microwave.

¼ cup finely chopped mixed peel
¼ cup Grand Marnier
20cm round Génoise Sponge
2 x 200g rolls marzipan
CREME PATISSIERE
1½ cups milk
3 egg yolks
⅓ cup castor sugar
1 tablespoon plain flour
1 tablespoon cornflour
1 teaspoon vanilla essence
SYRUP
½ cup water
⅓ cup sugar

China: Minton by Royal Doulton; linen: from Balmain Linen and Lace

1 Combine peel and Grand Marnier in a small bowl, cover, stand 2 hours; strain, reserve liquid. Add liquid to syrup. Add peel to one-third of the crème pâtissière.

2 Split sponge into 3 layers, place 1 layer on serving plate; brush with one-third of the orange syrup; spread with half the peel mixture.

3 Top with second layer of sponge. Brush with half the remaining

orange syrup, and remaining peel mixture then remaining sponge and remaining syrup. Cover cake all over with remaining crème pâtissière.

Knead the marzipan until smooth on surface lightly dusted with sifted icing sugar. Roll two-thirds of the marzipan to a circle, cut to a neat 20cm circle, place on top of cake. Roll out remaining marzipan; cut out 2 or 3 strips large enough to cover the side of cake. Decorate cake with wedges of glacé orange if desired.

Crème Pâtissière: Bring milk to the boil in saucepan. Combine yolks, sugar and flours in bowl, mix until smooth. Whisk hot milk into egg mixture, return mixture to saucepan, stir constantly over heat until mixture boils and thickens. Remove from heat, stir in essence; beat until smooth; cover surface with plastic wrap, cool to room temperature.

Syrup: Combine water and sugar in small saucepan, stir constantly over heat without boiling until sugar is dissolved. Bring to the boil, remove from heat; use while warm.

GENOISE SPONGE

This is a light textured type of sponge; the mixture is beaten over hot water to give volume and extra lightness. It is correct that plain flour is used. Melted butter should be cooled to room temperature before being added. The cake can be frozen for a month; it is unsuitable to microwave.

4 eggs
½ cup castor sugar
⅔ cup plain flour
60g butter, melted
125g dark chocolate, chopped
LIQUEUR CREAM
300ml carton thickened cream
1 tablespoon icing sugar
1 tablespoon Grand Marnier

3 Quickly and carefully fold in cooled melted butter. Pour mixture into prepared pan, bake in moderate oven for about 20 minutes or until sponge feels elastic to touch. Turn immediately onto wire rack to cool. Split sponge in half, join with some of the liqueur cream, cover cake with remaining liqueur cream. Decorate with rose petals and leaves.

1 Grease a deep 20cm round cake pan, line the base with paper; grease paper. Combine eggs and sugar in a large bowl, place over saucepan of simmering water. Do not allow water to touch base of bowl. Using a rotary beater or electric mixer, beat until mixture is thick and creamy, about 10 minutes. Remove the bowl from hot water, beat mixture until it returns to room temperature.

4 Melt chocolate over hot water, dip half of each rose petal in chocolate, place petals on foil covered tray; refrigerate until set.

5 Spread chocolate evenly over rose leaves, place on foil covered tray; refrigerate until set. Peel leaves away from chocolate.
Liqueur Cream: Beat cream and icing sugar until soft peaks form, fold in Grand Marnier.

2 Sift half the flour over egg mixture, carefully fold in flour, fold in remaining sifted flour.

Table: Freedom Furniture; china: Breath of Spring from Royal Doulton

2 Sift flour into large bowl, make well in centre. Pour in yeast mixture, butter mixture and eggs, mix with hand until well combined.

3 Scrape down side of bowl, cover bowl with plastic wrap and tea towel. Leave in a warm place for about 30 minutes or until dough is doubled in bulk. Beat again with hand until smooth and elastic. Spread evenly into a greased 24cm savarin pan, cover with plastic wrap and tea towel. Leave in a warm place for about 30 minutes or until dough has risen to top of pan.

4 Bake in hot oven for 5 minutes, reduce to moderate, bake further 15 minutes or until savarin feels firm to touch. Loosen edges, turn onto wire rack, place over a tray. Pour hot syrup over savarin, cool. Place savarin onto serving plate, pour over remaining syrup in tray until all syrup has been absorbed. Brush with glaze, fill centre with fruit and serve with cream.

Syrup: Combine water and sugar in a small saucepan, stir constantly over low heat without boiling until sugar is dissolved. Bring to the boil, reduce heat, simmer uncovered for 3 minutes. Remove from heat, add rum; stand a few minutes to cool slightly before pouring over savarin.

Apricot Glaze: Combine jam and rum in small saucepan, heat gently, stir until smooth, press through sieve; use while hot.

SAVARIN

The cooked Savarin can be frozen for up to 2 months. Thaw at room temperature, then wrap in foil, and reheat in a moderate oven for about 10 minutes. Remove from oven, pour hot syrup over the Savarin, cool, then brush with the hot apricot glaze. This recipe is unsuitable to microwave.

60g butter
3 teaspoons castor sugar
15g compressed yeast
¼ cup warm water
1¼ cups plain flour
2 eggs, lightly beaten
SYRUP
1 cup water
1 cup sugar
3 tablespoons dark rum
APRICOT GLAZE
½ cup apricot jam
2 tablespoons dark rum

1 Combine butter and sugar in a small bowl, beat with electric mixer until light and fluffy. Combine yeast and water in a bowl, stir until dissolved.

Furniture: Keyhole Furniture; china: Maddon Mall by Minton from Royal Doulton; linen: Hampshire and Loundes

CHOCOLATE SWIRL BAVAROIS

Bavarois and coulis can be made up to a day ahead; keep covered in refrigerator. This recipe is unsuitable to freeze.

½ cup castor sugar
3 egg yolks
1½ cups milk
3 teaspoons gelatine
¼ cup water
300ml carton thickened cream
60g dark chocolate, chopped
1 tablespoon water
2 teaspoons vanilla essence
RASPBERRY PASSIONFRUIT COULIS
250g fresh or frozen raspberries
1 passionfruit
1 tablespoon icing sugar,
     approximately

simmering water until mixture is pale and smooth. Heat milk in separate saucepan until very hot, quickly stir into egg mixture. Stir constantly over simmering water until custard is slightly thickened. Sprinkle gelatine over water, dissolve over hot water, stir into hot custard, cool to lukewarm. Fold in softly whipped cream.

1 Stir sugar and egg yolks in top of double saucepan or bowl over

2 Melt chocolate and water in bowl over hot water, stir in half the custard. Stir essence into remaining custard. Refrigerate mixtures until almost set, stir occasionally during refrigeration to prevent mixture setting around the edge of the bowl.

3 Swirl mixtures together in a large bowl, using a skewer. Carefully spoon into 4 lightly oiled dishes (1 cup capacity); refrigerate until set. Turn onto serving plates, serve with coulis.
Raspberry Passionfruit Coulis: Blend or process raspberries until smooth, strain. Stir in passionfruit and sifted icing sugar to taste.
     Serves 4.

BUCHE DE NÖEL

This cake is traditionally served at Christmas time; it is best made 6 hours before serving, then refrigerated before cutting. It will keep up to 3 days in the refrigerator. This recipe is not suitable to freeze or microwave.

3 eggs
½ cup castor sugar
⅓ cup cornflour
1 teaspoon baking powder
2 tablespoons cocoa
½ cup apricot jam
1 tablespoon brandy
½ cup thickened cream
FROSTING
100g dark chocolate, chopped
¼ cup castor sugar
¼ cup water
2 egg yolks
2 teaspoons cocoa
60g butter
½ cup thickened cream

gradually beat in sugar, beat until dissolved between each addition. Carefully fold in sifted cornflour, baking powder and cocoa. Pour mixture into prepared pan; bake in moderate oven for about 12 minutes or until sponge feels elastic to touch. Remove from oven, invert onto sheet of greaseproof paper that has been sprinkled with a little extra castor sugar. Peel lining paper from sponge. Roll from the short side, rolling the greaseproof paper inside, cool to room temperature. Unroll sponge, spread evenly with combined sieved jam and brandy, then spread with whipped cream, roll up again. Refrigerate roll several hours or overnight.

Cut a diagonal slice from the end of the roll. Place long piece of roll onto serving plate, press cut slice at side to represent branch of log. Refrigerate log while making frosting.

2 **Frosting:** Melt chocolate over hot water, cool, do not allow to set. Combine sugar and water in saucepan, stir over heat without boiling until the sugar is dissolved, bring to the boil, boil mixture uncovered for 2 minutes without stirring.

Beat egg yolks in small bowl with electric mixer until light and fluffy, gradually add hot syrup in a thin stream while motor is operating. Beat in chocolate and sifted cocoa, then softened butter. Refrigerate for about 30 minutes or until frosting is spreadable. Whip cream, stir in ¼ cup of the frosting; refrigerate until required.

1 Grease a 25cm x 30cm Swiss roll pan, line with greaseproof paper; grease paper.

Beat eggs in small bowl with electric mixer until thick and creamy,

3 Spread frosting over log, mark with fork to represent "bark". Spread cream and frosting mixture over ends of log. Refrigerate until required. Dust with icing sugar just before serving.

China: White Silk by Mikasa

FROZEN CHOCOLATE MOUSSE CAKE

This is a special type of cake; it is baked and then frozen until serving time. The cake and sauce can be frozen for a month. The cake is very rich with a heavy texture. Any fresh or frozen berries of your choice can be used in the sauce; we used a combination of strawberries and boysenberries. Serve small slices topped with berry sauce. This recipe is not suitable to microwave.

500g dark chocolate, chopped
155g unsalted butter
4 eggs
1 tablespoon castor sugar
1 tablespoon plain flour
BERRY SAUCE
500g berries
⅓ cup icing sugar

1 Line an ungreased deep 20cm round cake pan with greaseproof paper; do not grease paper. Melt combined chocolate and butter in heatproof bowl over hot water, cool to room temperature. Combine eggs and sugar in small bowl, beat with electric mixer until thick and creamy, fold in sifted flour. Transfer mixture to large bowl, fold in chocolate mixture.

2 Pour mixture into prepared pan, bake in moderate oven for about 20 minutes or until cake is crusty on top and soft in the centre. Leave cake to become cold in pan. Cover cake pan with foil, freeze for several hours or overnight. Just before serving, place cake pan in hot water to loosen cake; invert cake onto serving plate and fill centre with extra fresh fruit if desired. Serve with sauce and cream if desired.
Berry Sauce: Blend or process berries with icing sugar until smooth; strain.

NAPOLEON CAKE

We have given this French cake an "Australian" touch with apricot butter and passionfruit icing. Cake can be assembled several hours before serving. Apricot butter can be made several days ahead; keep covered in refrigerator. This recipe is not suitable to freeze or microwave.

2 sheets ready rolled puff pastry
SPONGE
3 eggs
½ cup castor sugar
¼ cup cornflour
¼ cup plain flour
¼ cup self-raising flour
APRICOT BUTTER
¾ cup dried apricots
1 cup castor sugar
60g butter
2 egg yolks
2 teaspoons grated lemon rind
MOCK CREAM
½ cup castor sugar
⅓ cup water
125g butter
PASSIONFRUIT ICING
1 cup icing sugar
1 teaspoon soft butter
1 passionfruit
1 tablespoon milk

1 Place 1 pastry sheet on oven tray, make small cuts over pastry to prevent pastry puffing too much. Bake in moderately hot oven 5 to 10 minutes or until lightly browned and crisp; repeat with remaining pastry sheet.

2 **Sponge:** Lightly grease a 23cm square slab pan. Beat eggs in small bowl with electric mixer until thick and creamy, gradually add sugar, beating well after each addition. Transfer mixture to large bowl, fold in sifted flours.

Pour into prepared pan, bake in moderate oven for about 30 minutes. Turn onto wire rack to cool.

3 **Apricot Butter:** Place apricots in saucepan, barely cover with water, bring to the boil, cover, reduce heat, simmer until apricots are tender; drain.

Process apricots with remaining ingredients until smooth. Return apricot mixture to saucepan, cook, stirring, over low heat until mixture is thick; cool to room temperature.

4 Place 1 sheet of pastry on board (puffy side down) spread evenly with half the apricot butter, then half the mock cream, top with sponge, spread with remaining apricot butter, and mock cream. Top with remaining pastry (puffy side up).

5 Trim cake with electric or sharp serrated knife. Top with passionfruit icing, cut when icing is set.

Mock Cream: Combine sugar and water in saucepan, stir over heat without boiling until sugar is dissolved. Bring to the boil, remove from heat, cool to room temperature. Beat butter in small bowl with electric mixer until it is as white as possible; gradually beat in sugar syrup in a thin stream while mixer is operating. Do not refrigerate this cream, or it will separate.

Passionfruit Icing: Combine sifted icing sugar, butter and passionfruit pulp in small heatproof bowl, add milk, mix to a stiff paste. Stir constantly over hot water until icing is spreadable.

Dresser, silver tray: Kerry Trollope Antiques; china: Juliet from Royal Doulton; linen: Balmain Linen and Lace

1 Beat egg white in small bowl with electric mixer until soft peaks form, add egg yolk then sugar gradually, beating well after each addition; beat until sugar is dissolved.

2 Combine lemon rind and coconut in bowl, stir in egg mixture.

3 Drop teaspoonfuls of mixture onto lightly greased oven trays, bake in moderately slow oven for about 10 minutes or until lightly browned, cool 1 minute before removing macaroons to wire rack to cool.

Makes about 30.

LEMON COCONUT MACAROONS

Macaroons can be made several days ahead; store in an airtight container. This recipe is unsuitable to freeze or microwave.

1 egg, separated
⅓ cup castor sugar
2 teaspoons grated lemon rind
1½ cups coconut

Chocolates can be made several days in advance; store covered in refrigerator. Small foil cases are available from specialty kitchen shops and department stores. Cointreau is an orange-flavoured liqueur. This recipe is unsuitable to freeze or microwave.

125g dark chocolate, chopped
1 orange
¼ cup castor sugar
¼ cup water
GANACHE
125g dark chocolate, chopped
2 tablespoons cream
15g butter
1 egg yolk
1 tablespoon Cointreau

1 Melt chocolate over hot water. Place a teaspoon of chocolate inside each foil case. Use a small spatula to spread chocolate around side of cases; refrigerate until set.

2 Fit a piping bag with a small fluted tube, fill bag with ganache, pipe into chocolate cases.

3 Cut rind from orange. Cut rind into small diamond shapes, as shown.

COINTREAU CHOCOLATES

Combine shapes in small saucepan with sugar and water. Stir constantly over heat without boiling until sugar is dissolved. Bring to the boil, reduce heat, simmer 1 minute without stirring. Strain rind through a fine sieve; cool. Top chocolates with orange shapes; refrigerate until set. Carefully peel the foil cases away from the chocolates before serving.
Ganache: Melt chocolate over hot water, stir in remaining ingredients, beat until thick. Stand 30 minutes at room temperature or until thick enough to pipe into chocolate cases.
Makes 30.

PETITE COFFEE MERINGUES

This recipe will make about 50 meringues so only pipe as many small ones as you require, use the rest of the mixture to make larger meringues. Cook these until they are crisp — around 1 hour. Meringues can be made weeks ahead and stored in an airtight container at room temperature. This recipe is not suitable to freeze or microwave.

1 egg white
½ teaspoon white vinegar
⅓ cup castor sugar
1 teaspoon icing sugar
2 tablespoons icing sugar, extra
2 teaspoons instant coffee powder
COFFEE CREAM
2 teaspoons instant coffee powder
1 tablespoon hot water
½ cup thickened cream

1 Combine egg white, vinegar and castor sugar in a small bowl, beat with electric mixer on high speed for about 10 minutes or until sugar is dissolved. Fold in sifted icing sugar. Lightly grease oven trays, dust lightly with cornflour, shake off excess cornflour. Use a 2cm cutter to mark rounds on trays to help keep meringues evenly shaped. Place meringue mixture into piping bag fitted with a small plain tube. Pipe rounds onto trays. Bake in a slow oven for about 40 minutes, or until crisp and dry. Cool on trays.

2 Join meringues together with coffee cream, dust with combined extra sifted icing sugar and coffee powder just before serving.

Coffee Cream: Dissolve coffee in hot water, cool, add to cream. Beat cream until firm peaks form.

TOFFEE-DIPPED FRUIT AND NUTS

Fruit and nuts can be toffee-dipped up to 1 hour before serving; the toffee will begin to soften after this time. The amount of toffee in this recipe is enough to coat about 30 pieces of fruit or nuts. For the fruit we used a mandarin broken into segments (do not pierce the membrane or remove the seeds as toffee will not cling); 2 glacé pineapple rings, each cut into 3 pieces, and 6 perfect strawberries. For the nuts we used unsalted brazil and macadamia nuts. Do not refrigerate dipped fruit and nuts. This recipe is not suitable to freeze or microwave.

1½ cups sugar
½ cup water

1 Insert toothpicks into fruit and nuts to make dipping easier. Combine sugar and water in saucepan, stir constantly over heat, without boiling, until sugar is dissolved. Bring to the boil, boil rapidly uncovered, without stirring, until syrup turns light golden brown.

2 Remove saucepan from heat, allow bubbles to subside. Drop a teaspoonful of the toffee into a cup of cold water. The toffee should set immediately, and break when snapped with fingers. If the toffee is not set, boil for about another minute before testing again. Dip fruit and nuts a piece at a time into the toffee, hold over toffee to drain away excess toffee. Place onto lightly oiled oven tray, stand at room temperature until toffee is set.

1 Beat egg white in small bowl with electric mixer until soft peaks form, gradually add sugar, beat until dissolved between each addition. Stir in sifted flour, then butter and essence.

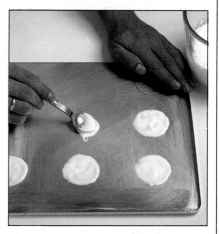

2 Place teaspoonfuls of mixture onto lightly greased oven trays. Use the back of the teaspoon to spread evenly into a 5cm circle. Sprinkle lightly with almonds. Bake in moderate oven for about 5 minutes or until lightly browned around the edges. Bake 1 tray at a time for easy handling.

3 Lift tuiles carefully and quickly from tray with a spatula, place immediately over rolling pin to cool. Continue with remaining mixture.
Makes about 20.

ALMOND TUILES

Tuiles are delightful to serve with desserts or coffee. Tuile translates as "roof tile", thus the curved shape of the biscuit. They will keep well in an airtight container in the refrigerator for several weeks. This recipe is unsuitable to freeze or microwave.

1 egg white
¼ cup castor sugar
2 tablespoons plain flour
30g butter, melted
½ teaspoon vanilla essence
⅓ cup chopped flaked almonds

China: Lily of the valley by Sasaki

Use your choice of jam in this recipe. Assemble pastry as close to serving time as possible. This recipe is not suitable to freeze or microwave.

375g packet puff pastry
¾ cup jam
300ml carton thickened cream
LEMON ICING
3 cups icing sugar
3 tablespoons milk
1 tablespoon lemon juice
CHOCOLATE ICING
½ cup icing sugar
1 tablespoon cocoa
1 tablespoon milk

MILLE-FEUILLE

1 Thaw pastry to room temperature. Divide pastry in half crossways; roll out each half on lightly floured surface to about 23cm x 30cm rectangle. Place pastry sheets on oven trays, prick with fork. Bake in hot oven for about 5 minutes or until golden brown and crisp. Turn onto wire rack to cool.

2 Spread jam evenly over flat side of 1 pastry sheet. Whip cream until firm, spread evenly over jam. Place remaining pastry, puffed side over cream, press down lightly with hand.

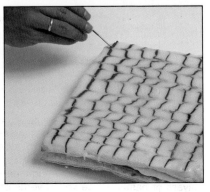

3 Spread lemon icing quickly over pastry, while icing is soft, quickly

pipe lines about 2cm apart of chocolate icing across lemon icing. Using a skewer draw lines at 2cm intervals in alternate directions to give feathered effect. When icing is set trim edges neatly with a serrated or electric knife.
Lemon Icing: Combine sifted icing sugar, milk and lemon juice in top of double saucepan or bowl, stir constantly over simmering water until icing is thin and spreadable.
Chocolate Icing: Combine sifted icing sugar and cocoa in a small bowl; gradually stir in milk, mix until smooth. Place into piping bag fitted with small plain piping tube.

1 Combine butter and sugar in small bowl, beat with electric mixer until light and fluffy. Add egg whites; beat until just combined. Stir in sifted flour with fork, stir until combined.

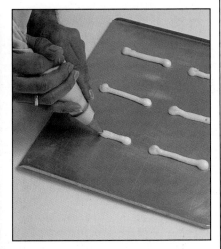

2 Place mixture into piping bag fitted with a small plain tube. Pipe 8cm strips onto lightly greased oven trays, as shown. Pipe about 6 biscuits on each tray, to allow for spreading.

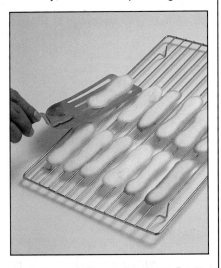

3 Bake in hot oven for about 5 minutes or until edges are lightly browned. Stand 1 minute before lifting onto wire racks to cool.
Makes about 24.

CATS' TONGUES

These biscuits will keep in an airtight container in the refrigerator for several weeks. This recipe is unsuitable to freeze or microwave.

60g butter
½ cup castor sugar
2 egg whites
5 tablespoons plain flour

Cushion: Australian East India Company

CREME FRAICHE

Any fruit of your choice can be served with this delicious cream. We selected pawpaw, pineapple, orange, tamarillo, kiwi fruit, blueberries, raspberries and strawberries. Serve platters of fruit with a knife and fork. This is enough cream for 6 serves; it can be made up to 1 week ahead; store covered in refrigerator. Framboise is a raspberry-flavoured liqueur; any liqueur of your choice can be used to flavour the crème.

300ml carton thickened cream
300g sour cream
1 tablespoon sugar, approximately
1 tablespoon Framboise

Combine cream and sour cream in bowl, cover, stand at room temperature until mixture has thickened. This can take 1 or 2 days depending on the temperature. Stir in enough sugar to sweeten to taste, then add the liqueur, cover, refrigerate before using.

Makes about 2½ cups.

China: Beaufort by Royal Worcester

MINI CREAM HORNS

It is important not to overgrease the cream horn tins or the oven trays; excess greasing will burn. Horns can be cooked several days in advance and stored in an airtight container. Fill horns with jam and cream just before serving. This recipe is not suitable to freeze or microwave.

375g packet puff pastry
1 egg, lightly beaten
300ml carton thickened cream
jam

1 Thaw pastry to room temperature. Cut pastry in half crossways. Roll out each half to a 25cm square; trim edges of pastry to give a 24cm square. Cut into 12 strips 2cm wide. Lightly grease cream horn tins. Brush each strip of pastry very lightly with egg.

Starting at point of tins, wind pastry around the tins with egg-dampened side away from tins; overlay edges of strips slightly, as shown.

2 Place horns on lightly greased oven trays. Bake in hot oven for 5 minutes, reduce heat to moderate, bake further 10 minutes or until horns are lightly browned and crisp.

3 Remove tins from horns, cool horns on a wire rack. Whip cream until firm. Place ½ teaspoon jam in each horn, spoon or pipe in cream.

Makes 24.

China: The Bay Tree

1 tablespoon finely chopped
    glacé cherries
¼ cup finely chopped glacé
    pineapple
¼ cup finely chopped glacé
    apricots
1 tablespoon brandy
150g white chocolate, chopped
15g butter
¼ cup thickened cream
¾ cup coconut
¾ cup finely chopped pistachio nuts
60g dark chocolate, chopped

CHOCOLATE PISTACHIO TRUFFLES

Truffles can be made up to 4 days ahead; store covered in refrigerator. To shell pistachio nuts: Place nuts in bowl of hot water, stand 5 minutes, drain, remove shell and brown skin; pat dry with absorbent paper. You will need 100g pistachio nuts. This recipe is unsuitable to freeze.

1 Combine cherries, pineapple, apricots and brandy in bowl, stand at least 1 hour. Melt white chocolate and butter in bowl over hot water, stir in cream, then coconut and fruit mixture.

2 Roll teaspoonfuls of mixture in nuts, refrigerate truffles until firm.

3 Melt dark chocolate over hot water. Spoon into a piping bag fitted with a small plain tube. Place truffles in rows, pipe chocolate over truffles. Pull truffles apart, refrigerate until set.
    Makes about 30.

INDEX

GLOSSARY

ARROWROOT: a thickening ingredient; cornflour can be substituted.

BICARBONATE OF SODA: baking soda

BUTTER: we used salted butter unless otherwise specified; a good quality cooking margarine can be used if preferred.

CHESTNUT SPREAD: an imported product available from gourmet delicatessens and some supermarkets; it is sweetened, flavoured pureed chestnuts.

CHICKEN: numbers indicate the weight, for example: No. 13 chicken weighs 1.3kg.

CORNFLOUR: cornstarch

CORN SYRUP: light or dark is available from gourmet delicatessens and some supermarkets; it is an imported product.

CREAM: we have specified thickened (whipping) cream when necessary in recipes, cream is simply a light pouring cream, also known as half 'n' half.

CUSTARD POWDER: pudding mix.

DARK CHOCOLATE: we used a good quality cooking chocolate.

DUCK: same as chicken sizes.

EGGPLANT: aubergine.

ESSENCE: extract.

FRESH HERBS: we have specified when to use fresh or dried herbs, or given alternative measurements when possible. We used dried (not ground) herbs in the proportion of 1:4 for fresh herbs, eg. 1 teaspoon dried herbs instead of 4 teaspoons (1 tablespoon) chopped fresh herbs.

GOLDEN SYRUP: maple/pancake syrup, honey can be substituted.

GREEN SHALLOTS: spring onions.

GROUND ALMONDS/HAZELNUTS: we used pre-packaged ground nuts in our recipes unless otherwise specified.

MIXED PEEL: a mixture of chopped crystallised citrus peel.

OIL: we used a light polyunsaturated salad oil unless otherwise specified.

PEPPERS: capsicum or bell peppers.

PIMIENTOS: canned or bottled peppers.

PLAIN FLOUR: all-purpose flour.

SELF-RAISING FLOUR: substitute plain (all-purpose) flour and powder in the proportion of ¾ metric cup plain flour to 2 level metric teaspoons baking powder, sift together several times before using. If using an 8oz measuring cup, use 1 cup plain flour to 2 teaspoons baking powder.

SOUR CREAM: a thick commercially cultured sour cream.

STOCK CUBE: equivalent to 1 teaspoon powdered bouillon.

SUGAR, CASTOR: fine granulated table or berry sugar.

SUGAR, CRYSTAL: use a coarse granulated table sugar.

SUGAR, ICING: confectioners' or powdered sugar. We used icing sugar mixture (not pure) in the recipes in this book.

TASTY CHEESE: use a hard good-tasting cheddar cheese.

VEGETABLES: we used all medium-sized vegetables in this book unless otherwise specified.

WINE: we used good quality red and white wines.

YEAST: allow 3 teaspoons (7g) dried granulated yeast to each 15g compressed yeast.

ZUCCHINI: courgette

OVEN TEMPERATURES

Electric Temperatures	Celsius	Fahrenheit
Very slow	120	250
Slow	150	300
Moderately slow	160-180	325-350
Moderate	190-200	375-400
Moderately hot	210-230	425-450
Hot	240-250	475-500
Very hot	260	525-550

Gas Temperatures	Celsius	Fahrenheit
Very slow	120	250
Slow	150	300
Moderately slow	160	325
Moderate	180	350
Moderately hot	190	375
Hot	200	400
Very hot	230	450

CUP CONVERSION CHART

	1 TBLS	1 CUP
Almonds, flaked		90g
Almonds, ground, slivered		125g
Almonds, kernels		155g
Apples, dried, chopped		125g
Apricots, dried, chopped		200g
Butter	15g	250g
Cherries, glacé, whole		200g
Cherries, glacé, chopped		100g
Choc Bits		155g
Cocoa		100g
Coconut, desiccated		90g
Coconut, flaked, shredded		60g
Cornflakes		30g
Currants		155g
Dates, chopped		155g
Flour, unsifted		155g
Ginger, crystallised, glacé, chopped		250g
Glacé apricots, chopped		250g
Glacé pineapple, chopped		250g
Golden syrup, treacle	30g	375g
Hazelnuts, whole		125g
Hazelnuts, ground		100g
Honey	30g	375g
Icing sugar, unsifted		125g
Liquid glucose (glucose syrup)	30g	345g
Mixed fruit, dried		185g
Mixed crushed nuts		125g
Mixed peel		220g
Peanuts, whole		125g
Peanuts, chopped		150g
Pecan nuts, chopped		125g
Prunes, chopped		220g
Raisins, chopped		155g
Rice, ground/rice flour		185g
Rice bubbles		30g
Rolled oats		90g
Sesame seeds		125g
Sugar, brown, firmly packed		250g
Sugar, castor, raw, crystal		250g
Sultanas		155g
Walnuts, chopped		100g
Wheatgerm		60g

NOTE: We have used large eggs with an average weight of 61g each in all recipes.